Conscious Wealth

The 30-Day Blueprint to Financial Freedom and an Abundance Mindset

Dr. Omar Clark Fisher

Conscious Wealth: The 30-day Roadmap to Financial Freedom and an Abundance Mindset
Copyright © 2021 Omar Clark Fisher
First published in 2021

Paperback: 978-1-922456-74-8
Hardcase: 978-1-922456-73-1
E-book: 978-1-922456-75-5

All rights reserved. No part of this book may be reproduced, stored in a retrieval system, or transmitted by any means (electronic, mechanical, photocopying, recording, or otherwise) without written permission from the author.

Because of the dynamic nature of the Internet, any web addresses or links contained in this book may have changed since publication and may no longer be valid. The information in this book is based on the author's experiences and opinions. The views expressed in this book are solely those of the author and do not necessarily reflect the views of the publisher; the publisher hereby disclaims any responsibility for them.

The author of this book does not dispense any form of medical, legal, financial, or technical advice either directly or indirectly. The intent of the author is solely to provide information of a general nature to help you in your quest for personal development and growth. In the event you use any of the information in this book, the author and the publisher assume no responsibility for your actions. If any form of expert assistance is required, the services of a competent professional should be sought.

Publishing information
Publishing, design, and production facilitated by Passionpreneur Publishing,
A division of Passionpreneur Organization Pty Ltd
ABN: 48640637529

www.PassionpreneurPublishing.com
Melbourne, VIC | Australia

Acknowledgments

This coaching playbook would not be complete without sincere acknowledgment to my mentors and teachers (both living and deceased) whose welcome advice propelled me forward, supported me during difficult times and offered shining role models worthy of imitation and emulation.

Among these are Bob Proctor, Jack Canfield, Mary Morrisey, Robin Sharma, Deepak Chopra, John Assaraf, Tony Robbins, Dean Graziosi, Vishen Lakhiani, John Maxwell, Tom Hopkins, Donald Meals, Wilford Welch, Wallace Wattles, Napoleon Hill, Jim Rohn, Earl Nightingale, Marc James Allen, and Raymond Holliwell.

The continuing love, care, and support from Salwa and our four children sustained me throughout this endeavor and cajoled me to accept the barrage of rapid technological and modern changes to almost everything including finance—disrupting what was familiar and comfortable to unlock real personal growth.

Quotes Worth Remembering

"The most important investment you can make is in yourself."
— Warren Buffett

"Never sacrifice happiness for the sake of achievement. The real key to life is to happily achieve."
— Robin Sharma

Call to Action

With this playbook, you have chosen me as your coach to deepen your understanding of money and finance, upgrade your skills and confidence in making financial decisions, and commence a journey towards everyday abundance thinking. Well done and congratulations! It is certainly an honor to work alongside you. An investment in yourself is always the <u>best</u> investment of your time and money.

To be more, do more, and have more, visit www.consciouswealth.me and join our community of like-minded people seeking to enrich their daily lives. Why wait? Seize the moment. We are here to support, guide, and coach you forward.

—**Dr. Omar Clark Fisher**

Contents

Chapter 1 — Introduction and Knowledge Partnership   **15**

   1.0 Introduction   15

   1.1 Program Rationale and Current Money Landscape   17

   1.2 3 Pillars Framework to the Roadmap   20

   1.3 Conscious Wealth Pedagogy and Approach to Financial Intelligence Learning   21

   1.4 Program Objectives   22

   1.5 Who is the Author and Why Listen?   27

   1.6 When it comes to teaching financial literacy, Conscious Wealth proposes new "best practices" as traditional methods are failing!   28

   1.7 Starting Point to My Financial Journey   29

   1.8 Chapter 1 Wrap Up – High Points Review   30

Chapter 2 — Taking Inventory   **33**

   2.0 What Are My Primary Outcomes of Chapter 2?   34

   2.1 Inventory   34

   2.2 Proven Tips and Process for High Achievers   37

   2.3 Abundance Mindset   38

   2.4 Chapter 2 Wrap Up – High Points Review   40

Chapter 3 — What Do I Really Want?   43

    3.0 What Are My Primary Outcomes of Chapter 3?   44

    3.1 Thinking into Results   46

    3.2 What do I really, really want?   50

    3.3 Often Roadblocks and Obstacles Prevent My Progress   51

    3.4 Key Concept: Your Mental Paradigm Controls Thinking   54

    3.5 Conscious Wealth: 14 Success Principles for Wealthy and Happy Living   56

    3.6 Chapter 3 Wrap Up – High Points review   58

Chapter 4 — Gap Analysis   61

    4.0 What Are My Primary Outcomes of Chapter 4?   62

    4.1 Gap Analysis Basics   63

    4.2 Define My Beliefs I Need to Hold to Advance   66

    4.3 Describe Beliefs I Must Have Now to Succeed   67

    4.4 Chapter 4 Wrap Up – High Points review   67

Chapter 5 — Role of Money   69

    5.0 What Are My Primary Outcomes of Chapter 5?   70

    5.1 Wheel of Life and Role of Finance   71

    5.2 Money IQ and EQ   73

    5.3 Within the scope of Money IQ, everyone has six main relations with money   74

    5.4 Added Bonus: Conventional Compared with Islamic Ideas of Finance   76

    5.5 Top 10 Money Relationships   77

5.6 Purposes of Savings — 80

5.7 Money Moods and Money Mindset — 82

5.8 Play the Empowering and Limiting Beliefs Card Game — 85

5.9 Chapter 5 Wrap Up – High Points review — 87

Chapter 6 — Finance Tools: Balance Sheet, Income, Cash Flow — 89

6.0 Financial Tools empowering Me to Conscious Wealth and Financial Freedom — 90

6.1 Why Learn About Cash Flow? — 91

6.2 What is a Balance Sheet? — 95

6.3 Elements of a Balance Sheet — 97

6.4 Major Threats to Savings — 99

6.5 Concluding Words to the Wise — 101

6.6 Chapter 6 Wrap Up – High Points review — 101

Chapter 7 — Budgeting — 103

7.0 Budgeting skills that lead to Conscious Wealth and Financial Freedom — 104

7.1 Sources and Uses of Money – 7x7 Magic Boxes — 105

7.2 Challenges to Consistent Budgeting — 112

7.3 Why does budgeting really matter? [for budgeting template refer to Appendix] — 112

7.4 Concluding Words to the Wise — 113

7.5 Chapter 7 Wrap Up – High Points Review — 114

Chapter 8 — Faith-based Values and Conscious Wealth — 117

8.0 Faith-based Values provide Guidance — 118

8.1 One Faith-Based Outlook—Everyone is Accountable for 5 Questions … 119

8.2 An Introduction to Conscious Wealth™ … 122

8.3 Assertion: Money is Not Wealth … 125

8.4 Grid of Wealth and Abundance Mindset … 126

8.5 Chapter 8 Wrap Up – High Points Review … 127

Chapter 9 — Goal Setting and Personal Financial Ratios … 129

9.0 What Are My Primary Outcomes of Chapter 9? … 130

9.1 Goal Setting … 131

9.2 Guidance to Goal Setting – Apply SMART Goals … 134

9.3 What do I really, really want? … 135

9.4 Improve Personal Decision-Making … 138

9.5 Personal Financial Ratios … 139

9.6 What do the financial ratios show me? … 140

9.7 Chapter 9 Wrap Up – High Points Review … 147

Chapter 10 — Retirement Lifestyle and Financial Freedom … 149

10.0 Retirement and Financial Freedom … 150

10.1 What Are My Primary Outcomes of Chapter 10? … 150

10.2 Imagine Lifestyle in Retirement … 151

10.3 Here is the Framework to Understand Financial Freedom … 152

10.4 World Wealth Report 2019 … 158

10.5 Meaning of Financial Freedom and Retirement Calculations … 160

10.6 Retirement realities exercise: use a calculator to figure how much should I save TODAY to retire at ease in the future. … 161

10.7 Chapter 10 Wrap Up – High Points Review ... 163

Chapter 11 — Pursuit of Happiness — 165

11.0 What Are My Primary Outcomes of Chapter 11? ... 166

11.1 Twin Goals: Failure vs Success ... 167

11.2 Pursuit of Happiness ... 173

11.3 Pursuit of Happiness: Common Beliefs ... 175

11.4 Happiness vs. Satisfaction ... 176

11.5 New Paradigm: Excellence in Living- Being Truly Fulfilled ... 178

11.6 Why Do We Struggle with Money? ... 182

11.7 Final Tips on the Art of Living Well ... 185

11.8 Chapter 11 Wrap Up – High Points review ... 186

Chapter 12 — Investing Basics — 189

12.0 What Are My Primary Outcomes of Chapter 12? ... 190

12.1 3 Ways to Build Real Wealth ... 191

12.2 Faith-based Values in Wealth ... 192

12.3 Wealth-Building Through Savings ... 193

12.4 Wealth-Building Through Investments ... 195

12.5 Wealth-Building through Investments-Trade Off Risk and Return ... 197

12.6 Digital Money ... 202

12.7 Chapter 12 Wrap Up – High Points Review ... 206

Chapter 13 — Gap Analysis — 209

13.0 What Are My Primary Outcomes of Chapter 13? ... 210

13.1 Gap Analysis Basics ... 211

    13.2 A Template to Consider Gaps   211

    13.3 Thinking into Results   213

    13.4 Chapter 13 Wrap Up – High Points Review   213

Chapter 14 — Action Agenda and Plan   215

    14.0 What Are My Primary Outcomes of Chapter 14?   216

    14.1 What is an Action Agenda?   216

    14.2 Potential Action Agenda Obstacles to Avoid   218

    14.3 Once Again, Concluding Words to the Wise   221

    14.4 Chapter 14 Wrap Up – High Points review   222

Chapter 15 — My Pledge   225

    15.0 What Are My Primary Outcomes of Chapter 15?   226

    15.1 How to Do My Pledge of Commitment   227

    15.2 Chapter 15 Wrap Up – High Points review   228

    CONCLUSION   231

Appendix   233

Web Resources Links   254

Reports and Articles   255

Bibliography   257

Index   261

Chapter 1

Introduction and Knowledge Partnership

1.0 Introduction

Less than 33% of Americans—the richest country in the world—have saved more than $100,000[1] towards retirement! The majority of millennials between the ages of 28-49 have managed to save less than $50,000. Consider that medical expenses over their retirement period are projected to exceed $200,000, so the promise of a "golden retirement" may be out of reach—or a myth! Adults across the MENA region are trapped in similar conditions; unable to save and invest.

Unless…

You regain control over your finances and apply the tools, tips, and skills presented in this playbook to begin regular savings. Time may still be on your side for making strides for wealth-building. Easy-to-follow templates, practical exercises, and cogent advice are combined within these pages to guide you towards financial intelligence: a growth mindset, enhanced confidence in financial decision-making, and inspired action in pursuit of sustained happiness.

The **Coaching Wheel Program** is about YOU and for YOU! The program is designed to facilitate YOU in achieving your goals and dreams because <u>success</u> can only be defined on YOUR terms.

---

[1] *Sources: Data from U.S. Census 2018 pegs savings at $50,000 or less, excluding value of their home.* **Median** *total household* **retirement savings** *among those working is approximately $57,000 among full-time workers, $23,000 among part-time workers and $71,000 among the self-employed./ www.annuity.org. TD AmeriTrade Survey 2019 and Federal Reserve study: "Report on the Economic Well-being of USA".*

Upon completion, you will have developed customized short-term and long-term goals, financial objectives (such as freedom from debts), prepared a realistic monthly budget, set saving and investment targets, and integrated all into a **Personal Wealth Plan** (PWP™). Why wait? You have the choice to begin this 15-Chapter program as self-paced learning or engage an experienced financial coach to enrich your learning.

The **Coaching Wheel Program** is my fourth book on finance and risk management. Since 1992, I have co-founded ten startups in equipment leasing, mutual insurance, business advisory, fintech, and education services. My curiosity about learning prompted me to earn a Master's degree in education with a focus on theories of cognitive learning in 1974 and follow that with a Master's degree in international business management (1979). During the past three decades, I have been regularly invited to deliver seminars at financial, insurance, and fintech international conferences and virtual webinars (see www.consciouswealth.me).

Any reader seeking a "get rich quick" program, or an off-the-shelf solution for their procrastination and self-doubt will be disappointed. The program will only deliver results if and when you, dear reader, resolve to do the work necessary; complete the exercises, case studies, and templates, and make the mental decisions and actions aligned with financial fitness. You will never get fit if your coach does <u>your</u> pushups for you!

Next is an invitation to you to get started—choose to expand your financial intelligence! In less than thirty days, a better version of you can emerge, armed with a complete blueprint for increased savings, well-being, and personal success!

Knowledge Partnership……

"To change your external reality towards your dreams, you must first change interior beliefs and habits to be aligned with these dreams."

Dr. Omar Fisher

Knowledge Partnership

You are amazing……

Congratulations on choosing to re-think your relationship with money and wealth! By taking the first step towards your most coveted dreams and goals, you are already on the way to completing your journey to personal financial intelligence: an essential tool for building wealth, sustained well-being, and personal success.

In starting this journey, you have completed 50% of the work required!

You are not alone. We are here to guide and support you every step of the way. The lessons, exercises, case studies, digital games, and other learning materials can be accomplished through self-paced learning or as a hybrid program that includes one-on-one coaching from me. This is entirely your choice.

This personal journey to financial freedom is designed as a roadmap to be fun, appealing, accessible, and easy to implement with ready-to-use templates. Let's get started!

1.1 Program Rationale and Current Money Landscape

It is increasingly obvious that most people today are working extremely hard for money whereas money should be working hard for them! There are two intertwined problems here:

1. We are working longer hours and more days per week just to pay our bills and maintain a minimum "comfortable" lifestyle, gradually becoming "slaves" to our earnings.

2. We are being fed a consumerist ideology that involves using our leisure hours to buy more material possessions that prove we have the "good life", yet even with all that money can buy, it is not providing the happiness we seek.

The pervasive consumer myth is that "more is better"; the more material goods we own, the better we can live and the better we will feel. In reality, this is a hollow truism. We strive for affluence and eagerly buy more because our warped concept of wealth dictates our wants, desires, and needs. We seem to have grown accustomed to buying everything and so we no longer live life—we consume it!

After all, many of life's simple pleasures are already free, and no true spiritual fulfillment can be purchased. Somehow, we have lost our way and the **roadmap** (our relationship to money and wealth) is either not available or needs to be updated.

The tools and techniques contained in this playbook will provide you with a new, revised roadmap—a **Personal Wealth Plan** (PWP)—that will allow you to redefine your relationship with money so it works harder for you. Your PWP will

2 in 1 Program

Personal Journey to Financial Intelligence, Wealth and Success
Coaching course has two (2) dimensions:
1. Instills confidence in financial decision making, upgrades skills, tools and methods for managing personal finance in practical ways.
2. Explores a values faith-based connection to Money and Wealth-building. Expands financial awareness within real world context of ethical savings & investing, increasing Conscious Wealth on personal level and assists with friendly financial planning templates to develop a Personal Wealth Plan (PWP) for the next 1-3 years.

What are My benefits & What can I learn?

	Specific topics examined during the course- as Self-paced and with Coach:
1.	Clarify my relationship with Money and the role of finance in my Life
2.	Make an Inventory of my Talents, Gifts, Assets & Liabilities
3.	Establish personal Goals and the connection with my finances
4.	Understanding the long-term consequences of Debts and how to reduce anxiety & stress
5.	How to boost personal Savings
6.	Become acquainted with tools of Budgeting and using templates develop my own Budget
7.	Orientation to faith-based values associated with Money
8.	Learn system for Goal-setting and enhance confidence in financial decision making
9.	Become familiar with important personal financial ratios banks use to assess me
10.	Reflect on my Retirement Lifestyle and the likely amount of Money required to live comfortably
11.	Understand the concept of Financial Freedom (FF) and calculate what is required of me to realize FF
12.	Define what is Happiness for me and become aware of how the Brain processes information as the Science of Happiness
13.	Familization with Investing Basics, what is my appetite for Risk and concepts of investment portfolio allocation
14.	Prepare an Action Agenda from a personalized template as guide for changing Money Habits
15.	Commit to a Personal Pledge for taking actions and making necessary changes to Money Habits to achieve my Goals

simultaneously alter your preconceived notions of wealth and allow you to achieve spiritual satisfaction by assuring your wealth-building actions and distribution are coherent and consistent with faith-based instructions. This program elucidates how real wealth is created and preserved, how wealth and risk can be managed on an individual basis, and how wealth is to be distributed in accordance with fundamental humane values and ethics.

Program Rationale

1.2 3 Pillars Framework to the Roadmap

Conscious Wealth offers basics in conventional financial literacy <u>plus</u> what is missing in education (shown in red).

Conventional offerings (black)

Conscious Wealth offers basics and what is missing (red)

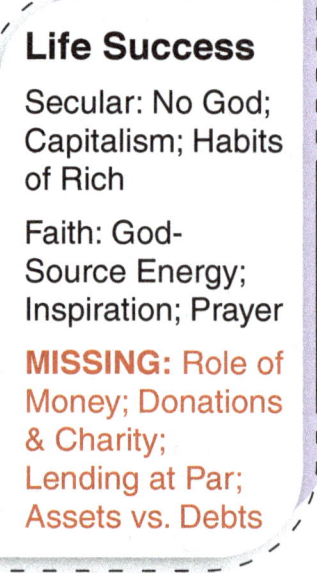
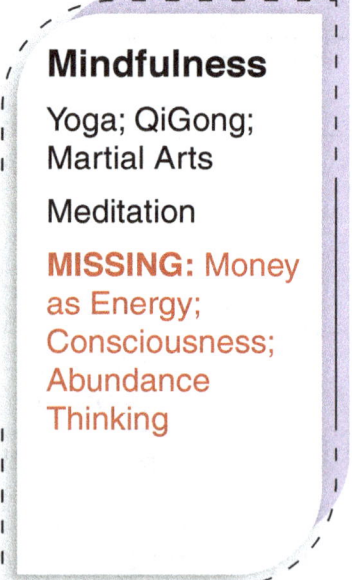

Finance
Conventional vs Islamic

FinLit – old schools methods

MISSING: Crypto-currency; Block Chain; Tokens; Cashless society

Life Success
Secular: No God; Capitalism; Habits of Rich

Faith: God-Source Energy; Inspiration; Prayer

MISSING: Role of Money; Donations & Charity; Lending at Par; Assets vs. Debts

Mindfulness
Yoga; QiGong; Martial Arts

Meditation

MISSING: Money as Energy; Consciousness; Abundance Thinking

1.3 Conscious Wealth Pedagogy and Approach to Financial Intelligence Learning

Approach

- Student-centric
- Coach is a guide to students' self-learning discovery
- Exercises, games, simulations, cases that make learning fun and practice reinforces that learning
- Action learning projects are essential to student comprehension, confidence, and long-term retention of new material

> All exercises, digital games, apps, and learning materials are learner-centric.
>
> The main focus is on Gen Z and Millennials.
>
> Learning is interactive, fun, appealing, and collaborative (synchronous), as well as self-paced (asynchronous).
>
> Curriculum development of lessons is modular and scalable for beginner, intermediate and advanced levels.
>
> Learners can experience a graduated user journey, earning points and badges, and qualify for Conscious Wealth Financial Intelligence Certificates (FIT ©).
>
> Learning pathways are ideal for at-home, after-work or school, Saturday money club, self-paced, or with expert coaching mentoring.

Learning Outcomes

1. Understand new financial concepts and money terminology
2. Build awareness and skills about money relations
3. Develop a **Personal Wealth Plan** for three years, and committing to personal financial objectives for 9-12 months
4. Explore the idea of abundance thinking
5. Use the roadmap resource and master personal finance

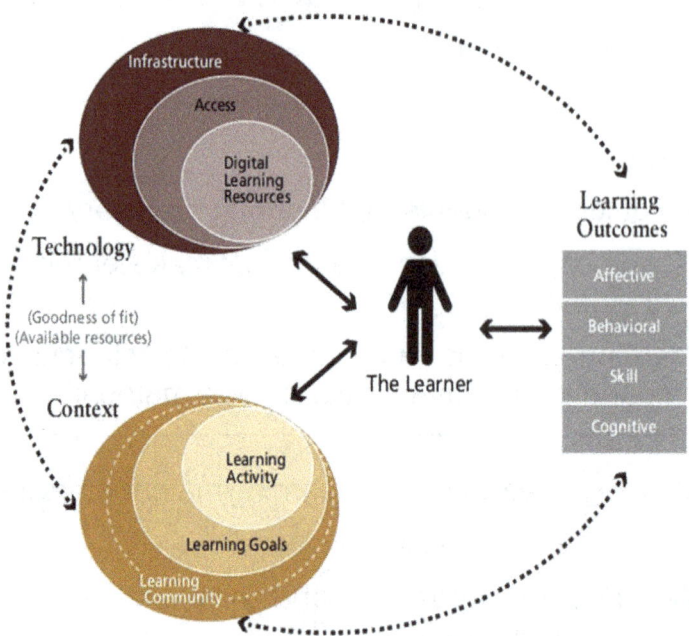

1.4 Program Objectives

- Have fun with money—it doesn't have to always be a boring, serious topic
- Be aware of money: know its role in your life, not only as a medium of exchange but in its value. How much does it take to be truly rich?
- Set financial objectives: how to control money and avoid accumulating too much debt
- Build skills and confidence using money tools: balance sheets; income statements; net worth; credit scores; first principles such as PayU first
- Gain clarity about faith-based values—what the Bible and Quran say about money i.e., the four dimensions: world vs. hereafter (dunia vs. akhirah); money builds character; integrity and donation; investor mindset relating to self and others
- Integrate the above learning through exercises and decisions to master personal finance

Exercise 1.4 – Identify My Primary Goal for this Coaching Program.

Pause and think about the "reason" I have sought out this program. What do I really wish to accomplish with this investment of my time, energy, and commitment?

Write down my **primary goal** so I can identify which existing money habit I wish to change. Now, briefly state it in the space below.

My money habit reset is: ....
....
....
....
....
....
....

At this early point, "how" to make this change may not be crystal clear—but that is not important just now. Instead, jot down "what" you desire to see modified in your current money habits.

Overview

This innovative Conscious Wealth Coaching Wheel Program consists of six steps:

Step 1: Building awareness and a desire to fulfill your personal potential

Step 2: Upgrading knowledge and basic financial skills

Step 3: Delving into goal setting and faith-based values about money

Step 4: Understanding financial freedom, setting retirement lifestyle goals, and discovering the concept of enduring happiness

Step 5: Basic investment orientation, learning to save and enhance risk-taking

Step 6: Finalizing a **Personal Wealth Plan** (PWP), **Action Agenda**, and **My Pledge** to implement them.

The next diagram shows these six steps in a graphic format.

6 Steps in My Blueprint to Conscious Wealth and Financial Freedom

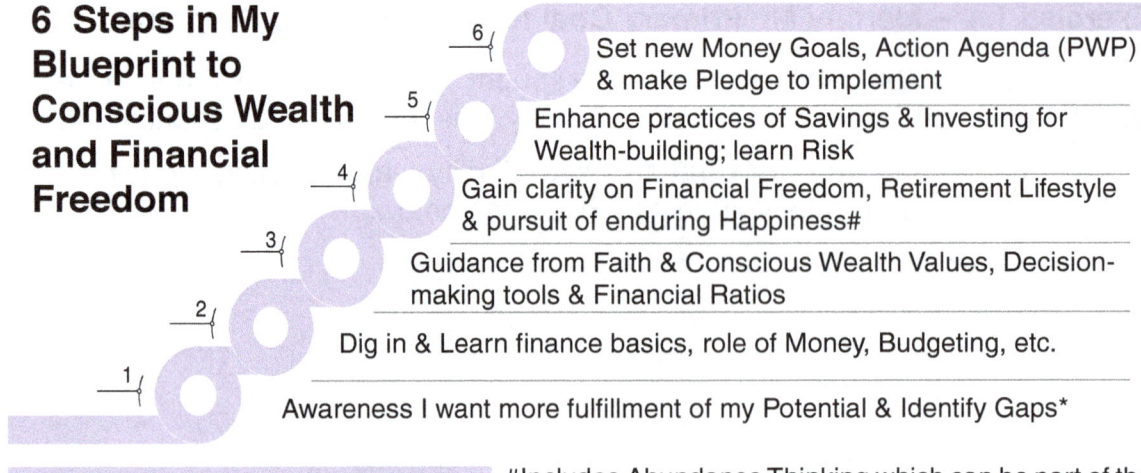

6. Set new Money Goals, Action Agenda (PWP) & make Pledge to implement
5. Enhance practices of Savings & Investing for Wealth-building; learn Risk
4. Gain clarity on Financial Freedom, Retirement Lifestyle & pursuit of enduring Happiness#
3. Guidance from Faith & Conscious Wealth Values, Decision-making tools & Financial Ratios
2. Dig in & Learn finance basics, role of Money, Budgeting, etc.
1. Awareness I want more fulfillment of my Potential & Identify Gaps*

** Use Exercises to help find the Gaps.

#Includes Abundance Thinking which can be part of the last or first Step in this personal Journey yet essential quality to consistent, never-ending Self improvement.

The 3 Conditions I Consent to when Undertaking this Coaching Program

Three conditions must exist to make the most of the precious time and effort I will be investing in reading and doing this program:

First, make a commitment to myself that I will read the entire program, do the exercises, and most importantly, put into action the PWP© that I select and design. Without sincere implementation, my plan will not change my current situation. Only by putting my savings, investment, and risk management decisions into practice can I hope to realize my goals and dreams.

Second, I must make a commitment to myself (or to a chosen financial planning advisor) that the personal financial information I disclose is an accurate, honest, and complete picture of my situation. Without objective information about my assets, liabilities, and other financial resources, the plan cannot provide me with the best possible guidance into the future.

Third, the concepts and methodology for this program are founded upon values and wise principles of original faith-based sources, such as the Bible, Quran, and Sunnah. To develop a proper attitude and understanding of wealth and risk management, it is preferred to become familiar with the valuable guidance provided in these ancient scriptures.

My Roadmap to Financial Intelligence

This Roadmap is designed with advanced finance games and education applications to make learning fun and engaging.

The Starting Point (Step 1) begins in this Chapter 1 (as shown in diagram) then spirals upwards into mastery of money and self-confidence.

The sections of the Coaching Wheel are design specifically to awaken knowledge, to teach finance skills, to engage with games and exercises so as to progress from your entry point to Financial Intelligence and Conscious Wealth.

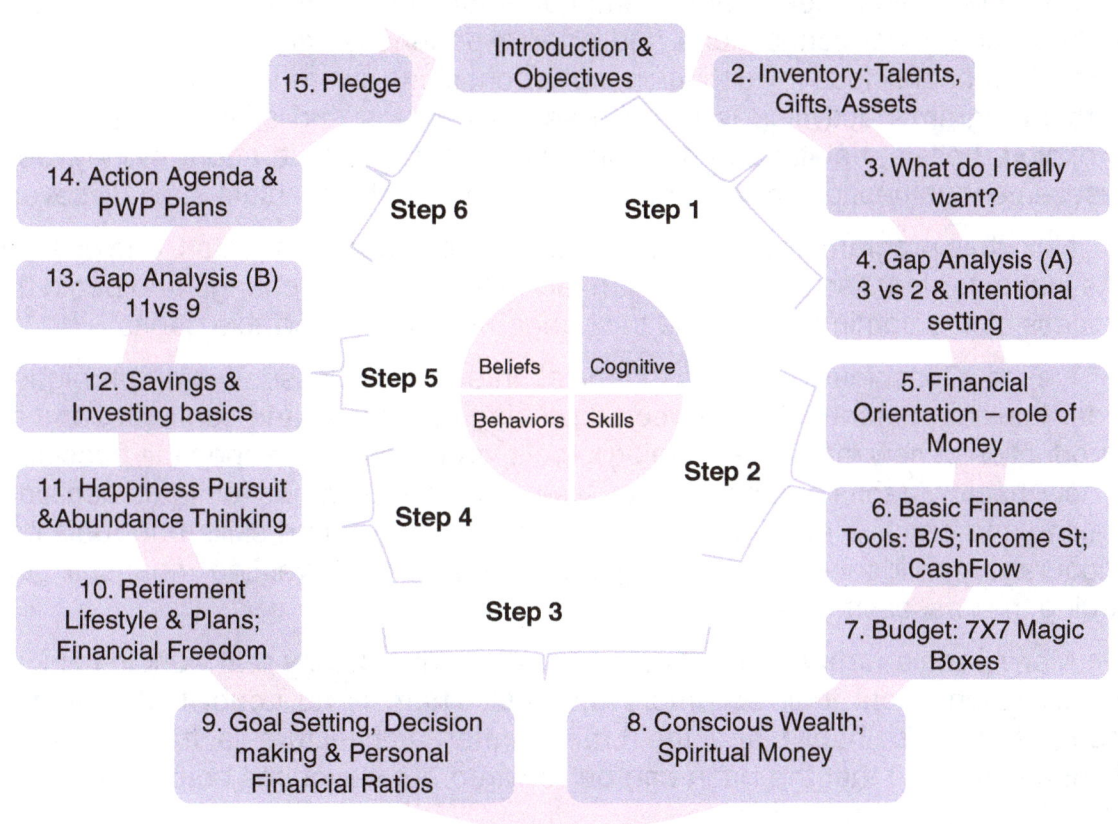

Benefits of this Coaching Wheel Program

There are three key benefits to this coaching program:
- Know yourself better and the manifold relationships you have with money
- Prepare a personal financial plan (maybe for the first time), customized to your primary goals.
- Gain direct access to a seasoned finance expert and one-on-one sessions that address your financial questions.

This Program Requires Higher-Order Intelligent Thinking

Most people have a deep-seated emotional attachment to money. Since many of these emotional connections and prior experiences with money reside in a person's subconscious (by definition, not a conscious awareness), a large portion of this program's activities is to build self-awareness and stimulate receptivity to explore beliefs, habits, and pre-conceived ideas you hold about money. Self-assessment games, exercises, and quizzes are used to stimulate such discovery.

Next, this program uses personal exercises, playbook templates, and one-on-one instructor-led discussions that can facilitate behavioral change and begin the process of overcoming resistance to change old and comfortable habits.

Hence Conscious Wealth's financial intelligence lessons aim at higher-order thinking, personal inner-directed probing of feelings and concepts, and an introduction of new money terminology, tools, and concepts to open the possibility of new, healthy habits around money. Case studies and games reinforce decision-making and practice at home (or online) of such new-found skills and tools can encourage confidence in managing money—savings, investing, financial goal setting, risk assessments, etc.

Many people want an "easy" pathway, refusing to do any real work in thinking deeply (even about their self-improvements). There is no doubt that changing thoughts, beliefs, habits and the brain's inner architecture is the real work. Science confirms that the brain can be re-wired but it requires commitment and persistence. Are you ready?

Conscious Wealth's Coaching Wheel Program makes use of all four dimensions of personal intelligence and growth:

The Coaching Wheel Program uses all 4 Dimensions of Personal Intelligence & Growth

Mental – rote learning, memorization, school conditioning

*Emotional – feelings, do I deserve this, empathy, connection, bonding

*Physical – repetition, bodily strength, peak performance, mastery

Spiritual – aspirations, passion, higher calling, calmness, fulfillment

Note* *Throughout Program these two are blended, so chief focus is: Mind, Body, Spirit.*

1.5 Who is the Author and Why Listen?

Every day, Dr. Omar practices daily gratitude and abundance thinking, while striving for peak performance and excellence in his various assignments and responsibilities. Yet, he is neither super-human nor a super-hero, rather, a normal person just like you.

Dr. Omar embraced meditation while in college and uses these quiet moments each day to deepen his inner peace and enhance awareness of transcendence. Beginning in the mid-1980s, he dedicated his time to learning about human consciousness and what causes peak performance: an uplifting blend of bodily fitness, mindfulness, and spiritual energy. Nearly four decades of such study is infused throughout this Coaching Wheel Program—benefits that are yours for the taking!

He is an avid sailor, hiker and lover of nature because it reminds him who we really are: "an eternal soul having a human experience". Like many of you, Dr. Omar struggled with money in his early years but discovered ways to impart basic finance skills to his children and went on to publish several books on risk management, leasing, mutual insurance, and the pursuit of happiness.

Resolve today to accept this offer from Dr. Omar to gain control over your finances, advance towards life success, and progress with mindfulness into abundance thinking. By standing on his shoulders, you can most certainly discover a brighter future!

1.6 When it comes to teaching financial literacy, Conscious Wealth proposes new "best practices" as traditional methods are failing!

Here is a quick comparison between Traditional and Conscious Wealth practices:

Traditional FinLit	Conscious Wealth - Gamification
• Few Lessons about Finance	• Broad array of topics on Finance & digital money
• Taught in classroom – large groups	• Webinars complemented by games, simulations, case studies and Action Learning Projects
• Teacher-led learning	• Mentor plus Self-paced learning (online)
• Dominant method is lecture & exercises	• Dominant method is experiential learning & discovery
• No basic life skills building	• Delivers Basic Life skills for lifetime
• Grading based upon memorization & recitation of "facts"	• Tests to help correct learning & emphasis on personal understanding & goal setting for success

1.7 Starting Point to My Financial Journey

Question: Why Design My Financial Life?

This simple question may never have occurred to you, yet it holds a grain of universal truth: if your life is characterized by too little wealth, you must first realize that in the absence of a clearly defined plan, your dreams and goals may never be achieved.

In most cases, the challenge is not to work harder but work smarter. All by itself: money is dumb. Money cannot make decisions or do anything to grow, it can only be directed and channeled by an intelligent human being into productive uses.

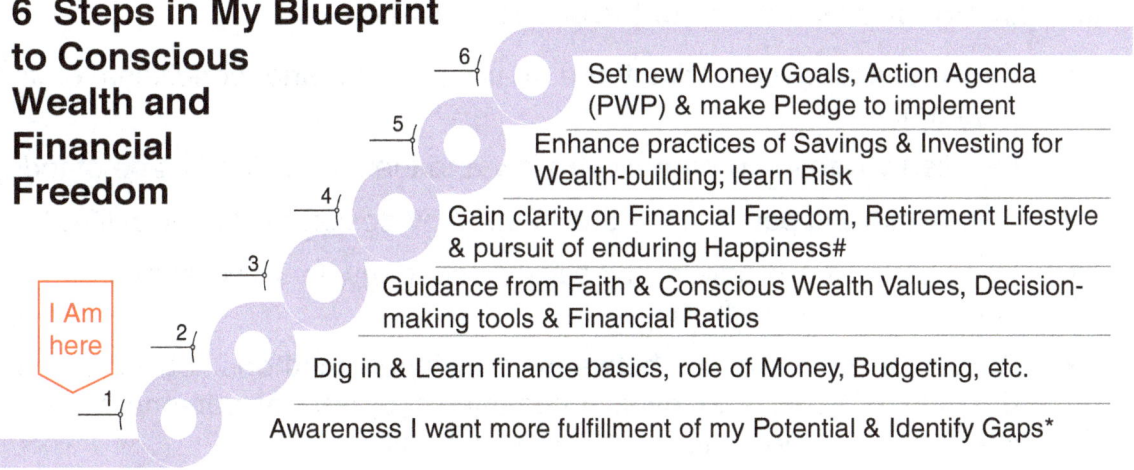

6 Steps in My Blueprint to Conscious Wealth and Financial Freedom

I Am here

6. Set new Money Goals, Action Agenda (PWP) & make Pledge to implement
5. Enhance practices of Savings & Investing for Wealth-building; learn Risk
4. Gain clarity on Financial Freedom, Retirement Lifestyle & pursuit of enduring Happiness#
3. Guidance from Faith & Conscious Wealth Values, Decision-making tools & Financial Ratios
2. Dig in & Learn finance basics, role of Money, Budgeting, etc.
1. Awareness I want more fulfillment of my Potential & Identify Gaps*

** Use Exercises to help find the Gaps.

#Includes Abundance Thinking which can be part of the last or first Step in this personal Journey yet essential quality to consistent, never-ending Self improvement.

1.8 Chapter 1 Wrap Up – High Points Review

Intended Learning Outcomes:
- Understanding the objectives of the financial intelligence program
- Getting clarity on the benefits of this Coaching Wheel Program
- Gaining awareness of the higher-order thinking embedded in the program
- Becoming familiar with Conscious Wealth's pedagogy and learning approach
- Digesting an overview of the program in graphic form and being comfortable with the 6 steps of the Coaching Wheel Program

Recap My Primary Outcomes of Introduction Chapter 1
- Become acquainted with three main benefits and conditions of this program.
- Familiarity with the program overview and the money landscape of today
- Find a "starting point" to the question: "Why design my financial life?"
- Understand the program objectives, pedagogy, learning approach, and how these can benefit me
- Deliver a comparison between traditional methods of FinLit and Conscious Wealth's innovative coaching program for personal financial intelligence—leading to healthy money habits

Chapter 1 End Note

Concluding each Chapter there is an opportunity to pause and reflect on the progress you are making.

AMAZING– YOU HAVE FINISHED CHAPTER 1 CONSISTING OF AN OVERVIEW AND ORIENTATION TO THE ENTIRE COACHING WHEEL PROGRAM.

WELL DONE!

NOW MOVING ON...THE NEXT CHAPTER IS A CRUCIAL PROCESS TO MAKE AN INVENTORY OF YOUR UNIQUE GIFTS, TALENTS AND ASSETS THAT ARE THE TRUE FOUNDATION OF YOUR JOURNEY TO FINANCIAL WEALTH AND PERSONAL SUCCESS. LET'S GET STARTED

conscious wealth

visit

www.consciouswealth.me

Chapter 2

Taking Inventory

Quotes worth remembering...

"There seems to be some perverse human characteristic that likes to make easy things difficult."

— **Warren Buffett**

"We grow fearless when we do the things we fear."

— **Robin Sharma**

"If you don't like the results you are getting, then avoid blaming others or making excuses, instead go within to closely examine your thinking patterns and smash any personal limitations you find there."

— **Dr. Omar Fisher**

At the beginning of each Chapter appears this image which identifies where I am now in my journey guided by my roadmap of six steps as shown below.

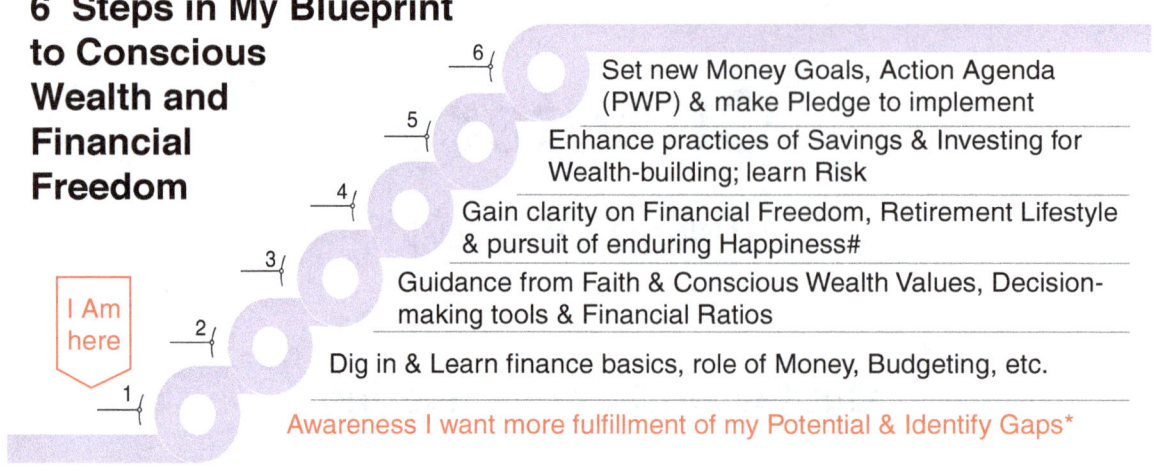

6 Steps in My Blueprint to Conscious Wealth and Financial Freedom

6. Set new Money Goals, Action Agenda (PWP) & make Pledge to implement
5. Enhance practices of Savings & Investing for Wealth-building; learn Risk
4. Gain clarity on Financial Freedom, Retirement Lifestyle & pursuit of enduring Happiness#
3. Guidance from Faith & Conscious Wealth Values, Decision-making tools & Financial Ratios
2. Dig in & Learn finance basics, role of Money, Budgeting, etc.
1. Awareness I want more fulfillment of my Potential & Identify Gaps*

I Am here

** Use Exercises to help find the Gaps.

#Includes Abundance Thinking which can be part of the last or first Step in this personal Journey yet essential quality to consistent, never-ending Self improvement.

2.0 What Are My Primary Outcomes of Chapter 2?

- Reflect on personal strengths, talents, gifts, and assets
- Prepare a written inventory of strengths, talents, gifts, and assets (use template 2.1)
- Deepen my understanding of differences between internal talents and gifts and external assets
- Trigger feelings of gratitude no matter how small or large the inventory is
- Establish a foundation for true goal setting to measure my progress

2.1 Inventory

Using the table below, write in your unique talents and gifts. Make this Inventory as long or as short as you prefer.

Inventory -1

Personal Strengths	Talents & Gifts
1. Aa	1. Cc
2. Bb	2. Bb
3. Cc	3. Ff

Now lets' examine these more closely. Ask yourself a simple question: Which would I like to have more of? (circle) Which could I have less of and be okay? (cross off)

Question: Which would I like to have more of? (circle) Which could I have less of and be OK? (cross off)

Personal Strengths	Talents & Gifts
1. Aa	1. Cc
2. Bb	2. Bb
3. Cc	3. Ff

Next make an Inventory of the existing personal Assets and Liabilities. Add the sum total of each column.

Inventory - 2

Personal assets	Personal debts/loans
1. Aa	1. Cc
2. Bb	2. Bb
3. Cc	3. Ff

Total Assets: _____   Total Liabilities: _____

Ask a similar question of your Assets and Liabilities: Which would I like to have more of? (circle) Which could I have less of and be okay? (cross off)

Question: Which would I like to have more of? (circle) Which could I have less of and be OK? (cross off)

Personal assets	Personal debts/loans
1. Aa	1. Cc
2. Bb	2. Bb
3. Cc	3. Ff

Next question. Do you currently have a written wealth plan? If not, why not?

Complete the next exercise worksheet.

Question: Do I presently have a Personal Wealth Plan (say for next 1-3 years?) Is it written down?

- A. No, not yet.
- A. What is PWP?
- A _____

- A. Yes, I have prepared a PWP.
- A. Timeline is [1/3/5] years out.
- A._____

> **Possible Answers:**
> Option 1. Use the Conscious Wealth Template to prepare a PWP.
> Option 2. Postpone preparation of a PWP until Chapter 14. Action Plans.
> Option 3. My PWP is attached to this Conscious Wealth Coaching Workbook.
> Option 4. I don't need a PWP. Hence, do nothing.

2.2 Proven Tips and Process for High Achievers

7 Keys to Personal Success with this Program

- Be aware of inner self-talk
- Control the direction of thoughts and vibration of thinking (+/-)
- Maintain faith; feel positive
- Realize "I become what you focus on"; so notice what you are thinking about and how you show up in the world
- Affirm that progress and personal growth equals happiness
- Your life as it is today is the sum of your previous choices
- Learn and practice Abundance Thinking (Chapter 11)

Conscious Wealth's Proven Process for High Achievers

- Assessment & Self-Evaluation (Chapters 2-4)
- Building basic Understandings & Tools for Personal Finance & Growth (Chapters 5-8)
- Charting new RoadMap, Milestones & Goals – Personal Wealth Plan (Chapters 13-14)
- Feedback & Measurement of progress – use of Accountability Buddy (Chapters 14-15)

2.3 Abundance Mindset

Guidance on how to adopt Abundance Thinking.

Realize that Abundance Thinking is different than knowledge and financial skills. Moreover, it is more than the law of attraction (see the film *The Secret*) because:

- Knowledge alone without application is only potential power, not real power
- Skills without finance and money are important in today's complex banking environment due to:
  - Money going cashless
  - Money is attracted not really "earned"—giving more value than price paid
- Must learn and apply the language of finance—glossary, instruments, securities
- Learn to earn and nurture multiple sources of income. This results in increased confidence in financial decision-making and progression toward financial freedom

EXERCISE 2.1

Read and reflect upon:

- The White Paper entitled: "How to Adopt Prosperity Thinking" by Dr. Omar Fisher, (2019)
- Worksheet by Marisa Peerce, 5 Steps to Practice Abundance Thinking (2020)
- Paper "10X Your Happiness" by Sandy Gilad (2015)

***Note:** refer to more materials in Chapter 11.*

Important Note: The following is a proven process to influence behavioral Habits which always needs consistent Personal Actions and practice*. To execute on behavioral change, here are the main points:

- Readiness to change: a willingness to take personal action; do self-analysis; make decisions that align with incentives (item four below)
- Awareness of what to change: information gathering; self-analysis to identify "gaps"; identify pros and cons; set a plan and personal strategy to move forward
- Resolving barriers: coping with inevitable challenges; obstacles to change; dealing with mistakes and disappointment; experiment with small changes; practice, practice, practice
- Network of support and incentives: develop key support eco-system—relations that assist and support; top/down; inside/out; focus on doing things right; mobilize resources to help in resolving frustrations; overcome "failures" quickly

***Note:** Process is not automatic. Individual results are determined by individual actions—you must do the work. However, individuals can save up to ten years by learning from and using proven models of financial learning set out by masters.*

How to Adopt Abundance Thinking

EXERCISE 2.2

Perform a self-analysis using these questions:

- Do I feel joy on daily basis? Or only occasionally?
- Does a "show me the money" attitude dominant my thinking?
- Where am I now on the money/happiness grid today? Which quadrant was I in last week? (see Chapter 11)
- Where am I now on the spiritual evolution ladder? (see Chapter 11) Which part of the spiritual ladder was I on last month?

2.4 Chapter 2 Wrap Up – High Points Review

Intended Learning Outcomes:

- Preparation of a personal inventory of gifts, talents, and assets
- Gaining clarity on what actions and decisions I want LESS of and which I want MORE of
- 7 key benefits from this Coaching Wheel Program
- Understanding Abundance Thinking and how to adopt it
- Discover what is required to modify personal behavior and establish new habits

MARVELOUS – YOU HAVE FINISHED CHAPTER 2 WITH AN INVENTORY OF THE ASSETS (HUMAN AND CAPITAL) THAT YOU ALREADY POSSESS AS A FOUNDATION FOR ADVANCEMENT. WELL DONE!

NOW MOVING ON…THE NEXT CHAPTER IS A CRITICAL REVIEW OF WHAT YOU REALLY, REALLY WANT! WITHOUT GAINING CLARITY OF YOUR HEARTFELT DREAMS AND GOALS, THEN YOU LACK A COMPASS TO POINT YOU IN THE CORRECT DIRECTION.

conscious wealth

visit

www.consciouswealth.me

Chapter 3

What Do I Really Want?

Quotes worth remembering...

"I insist on a lot of time being spent, almost every day, to just sit and think. That is very uncommon in American business. I read and think. So I do more reading and thinking, and make less impulse decisions than most people in business."

— **Warren Buffett**

"Fill your brain with giant dreams so that there's no space for petty pursuits."

— **Robin Sharma**

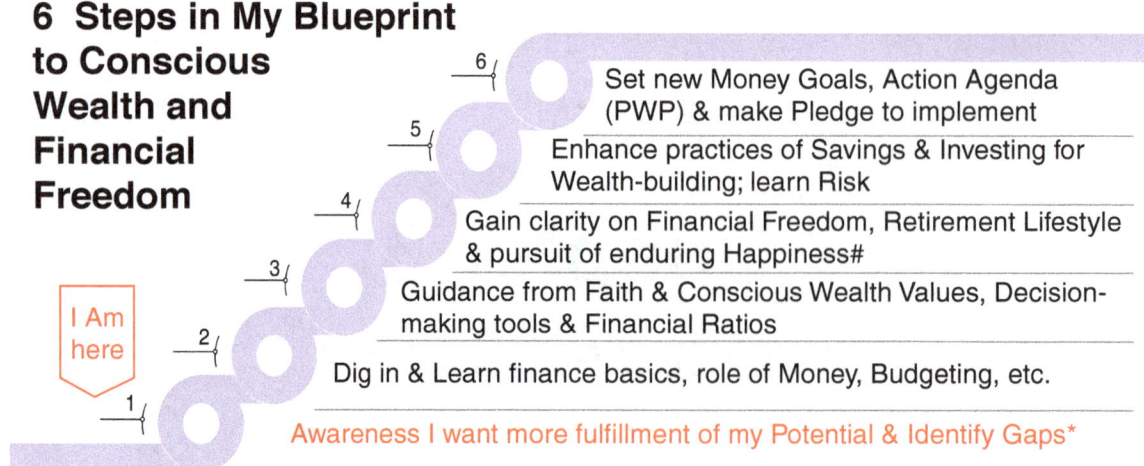

6 Steps in My Blueprint to Conscious Wealth and Financial Freedom

6. Set new Money Goals, Action Agenda (PWP) & make Pledge to implement
5. Enhance practices of Savings & Investing for Wealth-building; learn Risk
4. Gain clarity on Financial Freedom, Retirement Lifestyle & pursuit of enduring Happiness#
3. Guidance from Faith & Conscious Wealth Values, Decision-making tools & Financial Ratios
2. Dig in & Learn finance basics, role of Money, Budgeting, etc.
1. Awareness I want more fulfillment of my Potential & Identify Gaps*

I Am here

** Use Exercises to help find the Gaps.

#Includes Abundance Thinking which can be part of the last or first Step in this personal Journey yet essential quality to consistent, never-ending Self improvement.

3.0 What Are My Primary Outcomes of Chapter 3?

- Take time out to reflect on my true nature and purpose
- Drop all personal limitations and then project into my ideal future
- (Re)Discover true meaning and purpose in my life
- Begin finding a personal center for inner peace and contentment (mainly by reducing the perceived importance, judgments and opinions of others)

Here is an important Starting Point, a direct question in fact:

WHO exactly is thinking my thoughts? Who is the "**YOU**" behind the physical body, the mental outlook, the behavioral patterns, and the embedded soul?

Let's call this the composite **SELF**.

This SELF is living, breathing and contains thoughts. Yet where and what is the Life Force that is doing these things (for me)?

Starting Point: Who am I now?

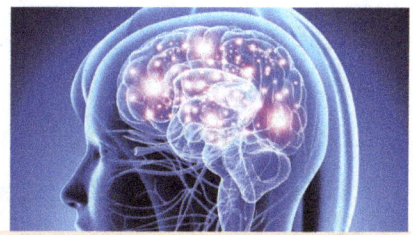

- WHO exactly in thinking my thoughts? Who is the "YOU" behind the physical body, the mental outlook, the behavior patterns and the embedded Soul?

- Origin of this "I AM" is a mystery, as is its miraculous functioning in each of us. Yet what is abundantly clear is that each individual when awake makes choices moment to moment on WHO I wish to become. Some choices are decided by the Conscious and analytical Mind (10% brain matter), whereas other choices are decided by the SubConscious and instinctual Mind (90% brain matter) – according to modern neuroscience#.

One source is: www.livescience.com

When I am asleep or dreaming at night, WHO is sustaining the composite SELF?

The "I AM"—a stream of consciousness—is always present and seemingly in full control of the autonomic systems, the mental and emotional components, and the creative energy making plans for my future.

#One source is: www.livescience.com

Question: Do I believe in myself?

A simple, yet deceptive question. Most people will respond, "Yes, of course…"

However, their actions demonstrate otherwise. Most people have a degree of insecurity that prompts them to seek out the opinions of others and allow influencers to govern their decisions. Or people rely on "luck" to push them forward in life. Other people stay passive, trapped in their comfort zone, waiting for life to deliver good things.

Such beliefs drive habits that dictate daily behavior—no one is born with such habits. These are acquired habits; conditioned responses gained from environmental factors and parents who believe they are doing the "best" for their children.

Self-leadership and overcoming such conditioning begin with inner security and self-confidence.

Conclusion: I can affirm: Yes, I believe in myself.

This is what I really, really want.

And

I take 100% responsibility for my daily decisions. I accept the opportunity to take risks and enjoy the rewards.

3.1 Thinking into Results

How do successful people achieve results? Particularly, the results that they dream upon and seek out. Here are some views on how to realize the results you want.

Thinking into Results

"The stuff from which all things are made is a substance which thinks. A thought of form in this substance produces the form."

"There is one original formless substance from which all things are made. All the seemingly many elements are only different presentations of one element...and this stuff is thinking stuff. A thought held in it produces the form of the thought. Thought, in thinking substance, produces shapes. [A human being] is a thinking center, capable of original thought. If a person can communicate his thought to original thinking substance, they can cause the creation or formation of the thing they think about." Wattles. D. Wattles (The Science of Getting Rich – 1910)

"Whatever the mind can conceive and believe, it can achieve." Napoleon Hill

"There's a difference between wishing for something and being able to receive it. No one is ready for a thing, until they believe they can acquire it. The state of mind must be BELIEF, not mere hope or wish. Open-mindedness is essential for belief. Closed minds will not inspire faith, courage, and belief." Napoleon Hill Think and grow Rich - 1937

"The stuff from which all things are made is a substance which thinks. A thought of form in this substance produces the form."
— **Wattles. D. Wattles, *The Science of Getting Rich* (1910)**

"Whatever the mind can conceive and believe, it can achieve."
— **Napoleon Hill, *Think and Grow Rich* (1937)**

"There's a difference between WISHING for a thing and being READY to receive it. No one is ready for a thing, until [they] believe [they] can acquire it. The state of mind must be BELIEF, not mere hope or wish. Open-mindedness is essential for belief. Closed minds do not inspire faith, courage, and belief."
— **Napoleon Hill, *Think and Grow Rich* (1937)**

Study this paragraph on the unity of all things as quoted by Thomas Troward, *The Hidden Power and Other Papers Upon Mental Science* (1921)

"If once we realise this, and consider that the Life which flows into us from the Universal Life-Principle is at every moment new Life entirely undifferentiated to any particular purpose besides that of supporting our own individuality, and that it is therefore ours to externalise in any form we will, then we find that this manifestation of the eternal Life-Principle in ourselves is the standpoint from which we can control our surroundings …we must lean firmly on the central point of our own being and not on anything else."

Suggestion: I accept the unity and oneness of all things and anchor my deepest desires and wants in an unwavering belief in myself that I am capable of realizing such desires.

Again from Troward,

"Now the immense practical importance of this principle is that it affords the key to the great law that 'as a man thinks so he is'.

We are often asked why this should be, and the answer may be stated as follows: We know by personal experience that we realise our own livingness in two ways, by our power to act and our susceptibility to feel; and when we consider Spirit in the absolute we can only conceive of it as these two modes of livingness carried to infinity. This, therefore, means infinite susceptibility. There can be no question as to the degree of sensitiveness, for Spirit *is* sensitiveness, and is thus infinitely plastic to the slightest touch that is brought to bear upon it; and hence every thought we formulate sends its vibrating currents out into the infinite of Spirit, producing there currents of like quality but of far vaster power.

But Spirit in the Infinite is the Creative Power of the universe, and the impact of our thought upon it thus sets in motion a veritable creative force. And if this law holds good of one thought it holds good of all, and hence we are continually creating for ourselves a world of surroundings which accurately reproduces the complexion of our own thoughts. Persistent thoughts will naturally produce a greater external effect than casual ones not centred upon any particular object. Scattered thoughts which recognise no principle of unity will fail to reproduce any principle of unity. The thought that we are weak and have no power over circumstances results in inability to control circumstances, and the thought of power produces power." Page 12

"We often do not sufficiently recognise the truth of Walt Whitman's pithy saying, 'I am not all contained between my hat and my boots', and forget the two-fold nature of the 'I AM', that it is at once both the manifested and the unmanifested, the universal and the individual.

By losing sight of this truth, we surround ourselves with limitations; we see only part of the self, and then we are surprised that the part fails to do the work of the whole. Factors crop up on which we had not reckoned, and we wonder where they come from, and do not understand that they necessarily arise from that great unity in which we are all included."

"'I am, therefore I can, therefore I will', the 'I AM' with which the series starts is a being who, so to speak, has his head in heaven and his feet upon the earth, a perfect unity, and with a range of ideas far transcending the little ideas which are limited by the requirements of a day or an hour."

"There are not two I AMs, but one I am. Whatever, therefore, I can conceive the Great Universal Life Principle to be, that I am. Let us try fully to realise what this means. Can you conceive the Great Originating and Sustaining Life Principle of the whole universe as poor, weak, sordid, miserable, jealous, angry, anxious, uncertain, or in any other way limited? We know that this is impossible. Then because the I AM is one it is equally untrue of ourselves. Learn first to distinguish the true self that you are from the mental and physical processes which it throws forth as the instruments of its expression, and then learn that this self controls these instruments, and not vice versa. As we advance in this knowledge, we know ourselves to be unlimited, and that, in the miniature world, whose center we are, we ourselves are the very same overflowing of joyous livingness that the Great Life Spirit is in the Great All. The I AM is One."

To realize My Desires and Wants what do I need to do?

One way forward is to seek mental clarity.

Realizing my Desires & Wants requires focus and clarity of Mind

How to achieve Clarity of Mind

- Single point of main focus (avoid distractions & multi-tasking)
- Acknowledge that what I focus upon expands & grows
- Shifting focus allows doubts & confusion to creep in this can weaken or delay forward progress
- Use affirmations daily to help establish a positive state of Mind
- Use visualization with some details to engage feelings/emotions and infuse emotions into the Images of Desire

Without a single mindedness about my Dream or Goal, the thinking mind jumps from subject to subject and may reflect conflicting goals. This confusion makes it harder to advance towards the priorities that are really important. When this happens, try this.

How to achieve clarity of mind:
- Single point of focus (avoid distractions and multi-tasking)
- Acknowledge that what I focus upon expands and grows
- Shifting focus allows doubts and confusion to creep in; this can weaken or delay forward progress
- Use daily affirmations to establish a positive state of mind
- Use detailed visualization to engage feelings and emotions, and infuse emotions into the images of desire

Raymond Holliwell, *Working With The Law* (1939)

"Form clear and definite ideas regarding your convictions as to why you do what you do, and as to why you think as you think. The practice of clear thinking tends to clarify the mind, tones up the faculties, sharpens the perceptions, and gives one a stronger and better grasp of the basic essentials for a larger and richer life ... a line of distinction, however, should be drawn between surface thought, that is, ordinary, trivial and commonplace thinking, and real thought, which is associated with the understanding of Truth. The latter is deep thinking, which arouses dormant powers, quickens the perceptions, and leads to the enlargement of the human understanding."

"Those who reach decisions promptly and definitely, know what they want, and generally get it. The leaders in every walk of life decide quickly, and firmly. That is the major reason why they are leaders. The world has a habit of making room for the [person] whose words and actions show [they] know where [they] are going."

— **Napoleon Hill, *Think and Grow Rich* (1937)**

Hill interviewed more than five hundred persons over twenty years to arrive at these insights and presented them in his personal development book.

3.2 What do I really, really want?

Exercise 3.1:

Question: If right now I had all the money in the world, I could be located anywhere, doing anything I wanted, then I ask myself, "What am I doing? Where am I? Who am I becoming?"

Exercise: What do I really really Want?

Exercise:

Use your Imagination…the most powerful mental faculty and instrument we humans have been gifted with…in your Mind's Eye what is the future you see for yourself?

See that new "Reality" as if on a screen (inside the forehead of the Mind). Now jump into that picture, you are now living that set of Images. How does this make you FEEL? What relationships do you now have? Who is with you? Where in the world are you? What exactly are you doing?

Here there are no limitations. No judgments by Others who or what you should be, or any feelings of being unworthy. Here you deserve all that simply flows to you and around you.

Write down these images as a positive statement of (1) my Purpose and WHO I want to become, and (2) the Things that I really really really Desire.

Write down these images that come up on the screen of my mind as a positive statement of (1) my purpose and **WHO** I want to become, and (2) the things that I really, really, really desire.

3.3 Often Roadblocks and Obstacles Prevent My Progress

*Note these are <u>primary</u> types of obstacles and failures only

1. Lack of well-defined purpose
2. Lack of ambition
3. Insufficient education
4. Lack of self-discipline
5. Poor health
6. Unfavorable childhood environment
7. Procrastination

8. Lack of persistence
9. Lack of controlled sexual urges
10. A desire for "something for nothing"
11. Poor decision-making skills
12. Controlled by one or more basic fears
13. Marital problems
14. Overly cautious
15. Toxic work environment
16. Superstition and prejudice
17. Unfulfilling professional career
18. A poor concentration of efforts

*modified from Napoleon Hill, USA 1920-1930s.

30 Types of Failure*

Exercise:	Identify which types of Failure arises for me. Are these temporary conditions or permanent limitations? What can I do to overcome these?
	* Take note that only 2 of these 30 Types of Failure are genetic or occur at birth. All other Failures result from personal choices or lack of making a firm choice. As Tom Hopkins states: "Attitude determines Altitude." Mental attitude and outlook is crucial to your personal Success; so nurture and cultivate a Positive Forward- looking Abundance Mindset!

19. Habit of over-spending
20. Lack of enthusiasm
21. Intolerance

22. Intemperance
23. Inability to cooperate with others
24. Possession and use of power not acquired through self-efforts (desire for quick riches)
25. Intentional dishonesty
26. Egotism and vanity
27. Guessing instead of thinking
28. Lack of capital

If I identify any of the above indicators of "failure" then what can I do?

Consult Conscious Wealth's proven process for high achievers to modify my <u>thinking</u> so as to re-wire my habitual patterns of thinking which can eventually bring about new results. This process is displayed as a graphic image:

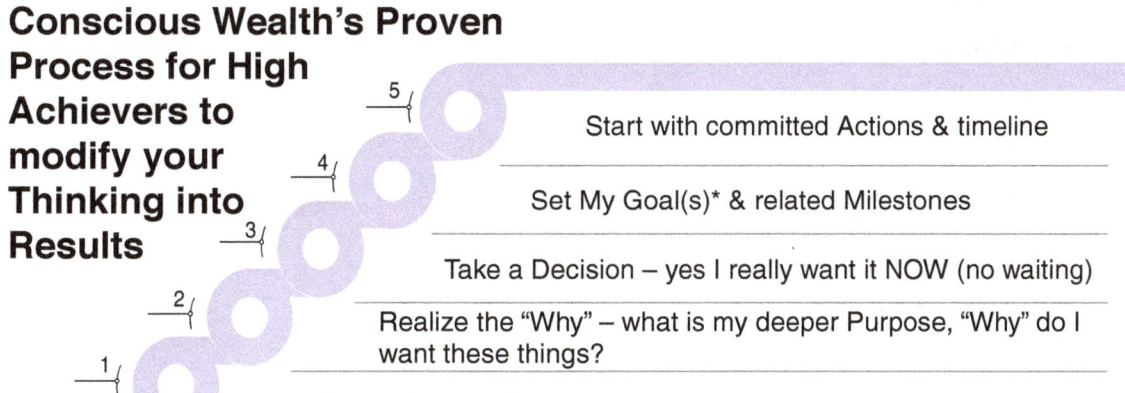

Conscious Wealth's Proven Process for High Achievers to modify your Thinking into Results

5. Start with committed Actions & timeline
4. Set My Goal(s)* & related Milestones
3. Take a Decision – yes I really want it NOW (no waiting)
2. Realize the "Why" – what is my deeper Purpose, "Why" do I want these things?
1. Mental Clarity & Focus on What I really Want

* Also, identify the resources, money, timetable, people etc that are necessary to attract into my present Reality to move this Goal forward.

3.4 Key Concept: Your Mental Paradigm Controls Thinking

Paradigm definition: "A *paradigm* is a standard, perspective, or set of ideas. A *paradigm* is a way of looking at something.[2]

The word **paradigm** derives from Greek and Latin and has been in use since the 15th century. In Greek, 'para' **meaning** 'beside' and 'deiknynai' **meaning** 'to display or show' were combined to form 'paradeiknyai', which possessed the **literal meaning** 'to display side by side'[3]

To understand your paradigm, look around you: all that you are, all that you have, all that you believe about yourself is this current day paradigm.

For the future to be different, your paradigm needs to change. Like a painting on a half-finished oil canvas, you are likely to only see similar results if you continue to paint the same way. You need to change the canvas, the paintbrush, and the images that your mind is presenting to you so that you can paint on a fresh canvas.

The Paradigm controls these seven main human faculties:

- Perception
- Use of Time
- Logic
- Productivity
- Effectiveness
- Ability to learn
- Ability to earn

---

[2] Vocabulary.com definition.
[3] https://www.macmillandictionaryblog.com/paradigm

Paradigm

Paradigm controls:
- Perception
- Use of Time
- Logic
- Productivity
- Effectiveness
- Ability to Learn
- Ability to Earn

```
Old Self  →  Paradigm / Difference is Awareness  →  New Self
```

Perception is a crucial main human faculty because it controls how we see our world. The brain is a "meaning making machine" and strive continuously to impress upon the reality we see perceived patterns and meaning. As a whole, these interact and produce your beliefs, your inner identity, and the limitations you may place upon yourself.

Change occurs not by blaming the paradigm, but by taking 100% responsibility for building new awareness, new patterns of thought, and new healthy habits (i.e., rewiring your brain).

So How Does Thinking relate to Money?

Firstly, money is an attitude.

Money is energy becoming vibrations that I think about and flows like a river/stream in two directions: upstream and downstream

Consciousness seems to flow like a stream; neither water nor I can go in two directions at once

I must choose my direction or the prevailing stream momentum will choose the direction for me

It is best to go "downstream" to be in a FLOW state and use the river current to enhance my personal power. The alternative is to go against the current—go "upstream"—where my power may be overthrown by circumstances, resulting in struggle, frustration, hardship, and feelings of being overwhelmed.

3.5 Conscious Wealth: 14 Success Principles for Wealthy and Happy Living

As an outcome of the author visiting for one week in 2018 with Jack Canfield, and his team, the master of self-development, here are success principles that are consolidated for easy recollection:

1. Take 100% Responsibility
2. Be clear in what I want
3. Believe in myself and believe it is possible
4. See what I want, and get what I see
5. Unleash the power of goal setting (Chapter 9)
6. Release the brakes
7. "Chunk" it down
8. Take action—start now
9. Just lean into it; feel the fear and do it anyway
10. Be willing to pay the price of persistence
11. Ask questions and utilize feedback
12. Keep score and commit to constant self-improvement
13. Rule of 5—practice and more practice!
14. Exceed expectations—give more!

*Note: Adapted from Jack Canfield's 64 Success Principles, *The Success Principles* (2015). More details about these **14 Success Principles** described in Dr. Omar Fisher's eBook (2020)

Concluding Words to the Wise

"The principles always work if you work the principles!" Jack Canfield

Don't blame the past; the past is perfect as it has brought you to this moment—poised for personal transformation. Be ready to learn more!

Celebrate a new awareness; change in personal habits is never easy. Our "old, comfortable self" constantly pulls us back into that familiar comfort zone. Yet, it is always possible to break through this familiarity and find new ways of doing things.

Try on the new wings—become free and liberated from past limitations and advance towards your true self.

Remember that success takes time and perseverance. This is not necessarily hard work, but steady, forward momentum into new habits and ideals, coping with inevitable challenges, changes, and obstacles, as well as dealing with disappointment and mistakes that arise. The key is determination and practice, practice, practice.

Develop a network of support: like any journey, going at it alone is tough, so choose friends, family, relatives, and colleagues who empathize with your desire for personal change and can form a support system to assist, offer advice, encouragement, and help mobilize resources, information and solutions to resolve frustrations and quickly overcome temporary "failures".

Note: this process is not automatic. Individual results are determined by individual actions—you must do the work. However, individuals can save up to ten years by learning from and using proven models of financial learning set out by masters.

3.6 Chapter 3 Wrap Up – High Points review

Intended Learning Outcomes:

- Clear-eyed description of what "I really, really want"
- Recommendations to believe in myself and achieve clarity of mind
- Explanation with examples of "thinking into results" with references to renowned authors
- Awareness of "paradigm" and how this influences my mind and patterns of behavior
- Introduction to 14 Success Principles as guidance to my achievement what I really, really want

FABULOUS! YOU HAVE COMPLETED CHAPTER 3 WHICH REVEALED OR UNCOVERED WHAT YOU DEEPLY DESIRE. SO 20% OF YOUR JOURNEY IS ACCOMPLISHED. WELL DONE!

NOW MOVING ON...THE NEXT CHAPTER GUIDES YOU THROUGH A GAP ANALYSIS TO COMPARE AND CONTRAST THE RESULTS OF YOUR CURRENT REALITY WITH THE FUTURE RESULTS YOU FORSEE. THIS CLARITY CAN GUIDE YOU TO SET MILESTONES AND IDENTIFY RESOURCES AND SKILLS REQUIRED TO REALIZE THE GOALS YOU ARE MOST PASSIONATE ABOUT.

conscious wealth

visit

www.consciouswealth.me

Chapter 4

Gap Analysis

Quotes worth remembering...

"In the world of business, the people who are most successful are those who are doing what they love."

— **Warren Buffett**

"Dream big, start small, act now."

— **Robin Sharma**

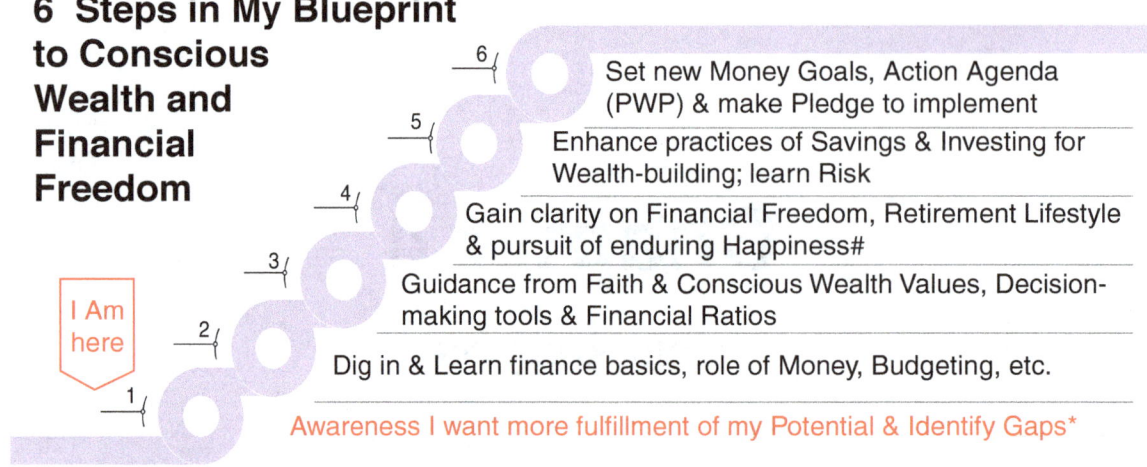

6 Steps in My Blueprint to Conscious Wealth and Financial Freedom

6. Set new Money Goals, Action Agenda (PWP) & make Pledge to implement
5. Enhance practices of Savings & Investing for Wealth-building; learn Risk
4. Gain clarity on Financial Freedom, Retirement Lifestyle & pursuit of enduring Happiness#
3. Guidance from Faith & Conscious Wealth Values, Decision-making tools & Financial Ratios
2. Dig in & Learn finance basics, role of Money, Budgeting, etc.
1. Awareness I want more fulfillment of my Potential & Identify Gaps*

I Am here

** Use Exercises to help find the Gaps.

#Includes Abundance Thinking which can be part of the last or first Step in this personal Journey yet essential quality to consistent, never-ending Self improvement.

4.0 What Are My Primary Outcomes of Chapter 4?

- Analyze outcomes from Chapter 3: What do I really, really want?
- Analyze outcomes from Chapter 2: Inventory of Gifts, Talents, and Assets.
- Compare these sets of outcomes. What gaps do I notice?

Examine carefully:

- Where am I placing my central focus on daily basis?
- Where am I having success in realizing the results that I seek?
- Where are the main obstacles to forward progress?
- Which areas are my skills and talents inadequate and must be improved, updated, or expanded?
- What additional resources—money, things, people, and experiences—are necessary to help close the gaps?

4.1 Gap Analysis Basics

Describe the reality of your current situation.

Describe your desired reality in detail… what is the ideal future you are moving towards?

When comparing these two pictures, what stands out as not aligned? What is aligned and yet not the anticipated quantity (i.e., not yet enough)?

Where are the gaps—the largest differences? The smallest differences?

A template from selling to help consider gaps

1. Stretch your imagination to identify the nature of the **gaps** and reflect on what can be done to narrow or fully close each **gap**.

2. Next, set priorities. Perhaps certain **gaps** will only be closed once other aspects have evolved. For example, running hurdles faster requires X number of hours of practice on the course for familiarization and augmenting courage.

3. If reducing certain **gaps** necessitates time and money, then allocate a budget to make that investment.

4. Recall that intentions must be anchored in commitment and actions to become part of your new reality. Wishful thinking is not enough.

A template from sales to help consider Gaps

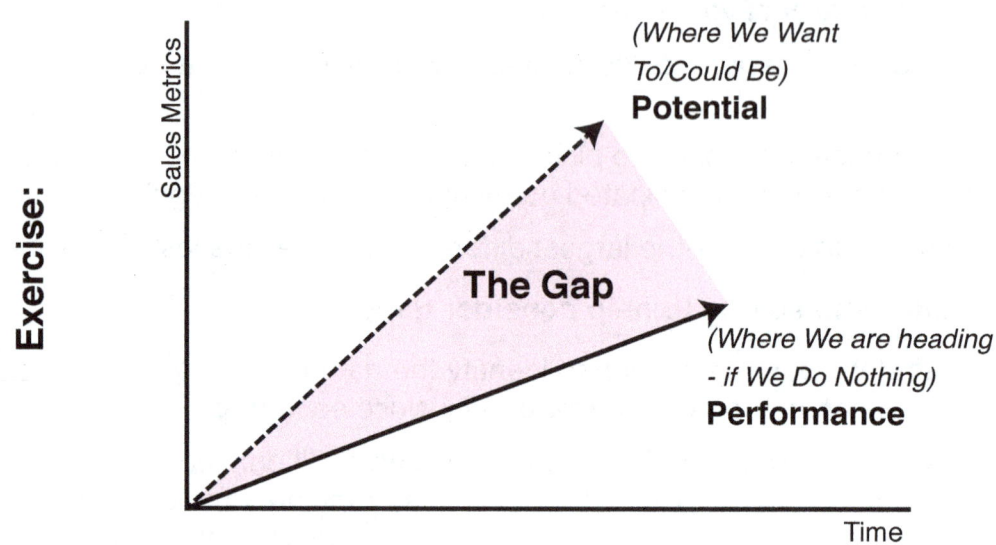

Case Study – Example of Gap Analysis

<u>Current State examples</u>

Earnings:	Monthly income: $6,000
Career:	Support function at work
Relations:	Single, no current steady partner Visit family/parents once per year
Health:	Weight is 77kg Exercise twice per week (total two hours)

<u>Desired Ideal State examples</u>

Earnings:	Monthly income: $12,000
Career:	Manage three or more staff members
Relations:	Seeking special partner for serious relationship and marriage Visit family/parents three times per year
Health:	Regime to reduce 5kg over next four months Exercise five times per week (total five hours)

Please note that there are four separate Quadrants to inspect:

Career / Family / Health / Spirit

Case Study – Example of Gap Analysis

Gaps to Close

- Monthly salary increase of $6,000
- Add new skills to qualify as a manager
- Describe ideal partner; speak to relatives and communities where this type of person may be found
- Set aside savings funds for travel and allocate holiday time in advance
- Research approved diets to lose weight
- Hire a personal trainer or stream online videos and resolve to schedule gym time or regular, early morning aerobics

Desired Ideal State

- Monthly income: $12,000
- Manage three or staff members
- Seeking special partner for serious relationship and marriage
- Visit family/parents three times per year
- Regime to reduce weight by 5kg over next four months
- Exercise five times per week (total five hours)

4.2 Define My Beliefs I Need to Hold to Advance

Define My Beliefs:

....
....
....
....
....
....
....
....
....

Next, identify the new beliefs that I must hold about myself, my environment, and my current reality to make me receptive to changes and make way for the new reality to arrive. This is the reaction in the law of attraction (a universal law) to me thinking my desires onto the formless substance.

To modify existing beliefs (established in infancy and early childhood) often takes time and practice to reset the brain patterns in support of the new desired reality. Stay committed and believe these changes can occur to reduce the gaps.

4.3 Describe Beliefs I Must Have Now to Succeed

Exercise

- **"I now believe that I am capable of** ....
...."

- **"I now believe that I can do** ....
...."

- **"I now believe that I deserve** ....
...."

- **"I now believe that I am worthy to have** ....
...."

- ....
....

- ....
....

- ....
....

4.4 Chapter 4 Wrap Up – High Points review

Intended Learning Outcomes:

- Performing a gap analysis on my current situation vs. my desired future situation

- Assessment of the areas where gaps exist to quantify what these gaps consistent of; namely, capital, skills, knowledge, commitment, motivation, etc.

- Prepare a plan with milestones and a timeline for addressing the gaps and pulling the desired future goals closer to my present-day reality (more on the plan in Chapter 14)

PAT YOURSELF ON THE BACK- YOU HAVE FINISHED CHAPTER 4 WITH A THOROUGH FIRST GAP ANALYSIS WHICH IS ESSENTIAL TO PLANNING CHANGES FOR A BRIGHTER FUTURE. WELL DONE!

NOW MOVING AHEAD...THE NEXT CHAPTER 5 IS A COMPREHENSIVE LOOK INTO THE ROLE OF MONEY AND FINANCE BASICS, AND HOW MONEY FITS INTO YOUR DAILY LIFE. THIS IS IMPORTANT FOUNDATION TO YOUR SELF-CONFIDENCE. SO LET'S PROCEED!

conscious wealth

visit

www.consciouswealth.me

Chapter 5

Role of Money

Quotes worth remembering...

"Of the billionaires I have known, money just brings out the basic traits in them. If they were jerks before they had money, they are simply jerks with a billion dollars."
— **Warren Buffett**

"You are born into genius, but have you resigned yourself to mediocrity?"
— **Robin Sharma**

6 Steps in My Blueprint to Conscious Wealth and Financial Freedom

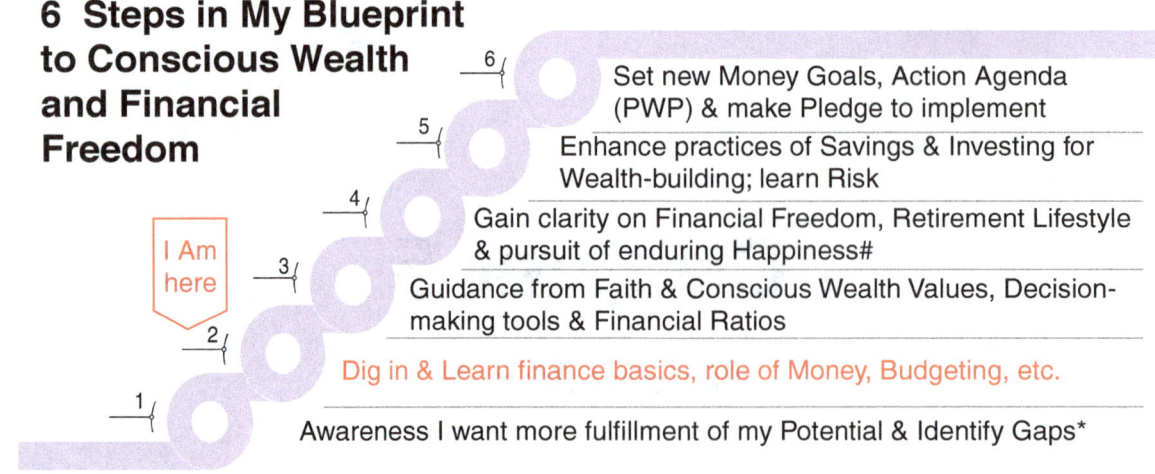

6. Set new Money Goals, Action Agenda (PWP) & make Pledge to implement
5. Enhance practices of Savings & Investing for Wealth-building; learn Risk
4. Gain clarity on Financial Freedom, Retirement Lifestyle & pursuit of enduring Happiness#
3. Guidance from Faith & Conscious Wealth Values, Decision-making tools & Financial Ratios
2. Dig in & Learn finance basics, role of Money, Budgeting, etc.
1. Awareness I want more fulfillment of my Potential & Identify Gaps*

I Am here

** Use Exercises to help find the Gaps.

#Includes Abundance Thinking which can be part of the last or first Step in this personal Journey yet essential quality to consistent, never-ending Self improvement.

5.0 What Are My Primary Outcomes of Chapter 5?

- Take the analysis outcomes from Chapter 4 above and begin to identify relationships to money and to finance
- Understand the role of money in my life using the Wheel of Life tool
- Understand the eight money functions and how these apply to my life
- Develop an overview of the vast range of money relationships (>36) that each person develops over her/his lifetime and the importance of sorting out the language and documentation of each (outside the scope of this program)
- Become aware of the five money mindset traps to avoid
- Perform an exercise of empowering and limiting beliefs to highlight personal areas of improvement and where behavior changes are needed

How Does Money and Finance Fit into My Life?

Answers to the above question includes the following components:

- Explore the "Wheel of Life" diagram and conduct the exercise to see where money belongs
- Identify the main activities and deployment of personal money
- Dig into personal money basics to examine sources and uses of capital
- Become familiar with a budget framework

5.1 Wheel of Life and Role of Finance

Exercise 5.1:

Key Questions: Where does finance fit into my life?

- Which sectors need money?
- Of the multiple methods to pay- which are cash or cashless?
- What is my cost of credit?
- Am I living debt-free?
- In which sector do I practice money fitness?

(Place your answers on the diagram below within each segment)

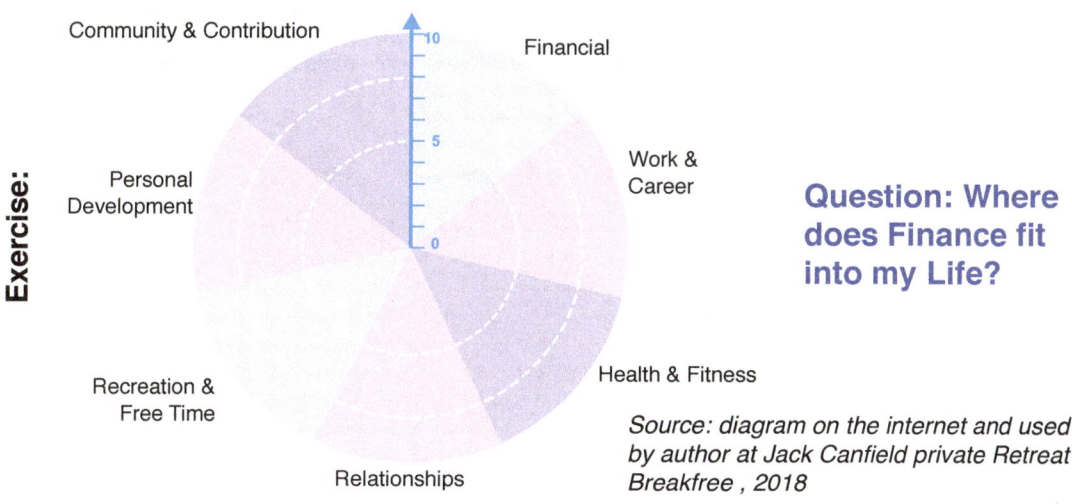

Source: diagram on the internet and used by author at Jack Canfield private Retreat Breakfree, 2018

Next use the same diagram and rate your level of satisfaction in these seven segments using 1 Low to 10 High.

Then make a note which segments are influenced by money—also rate these 1 Low to 10 High.

Exercise: Rate your level of Satisfaction in each 7 segments using 1 Low to 10 High.

YOUR WHEEL OF LIFE

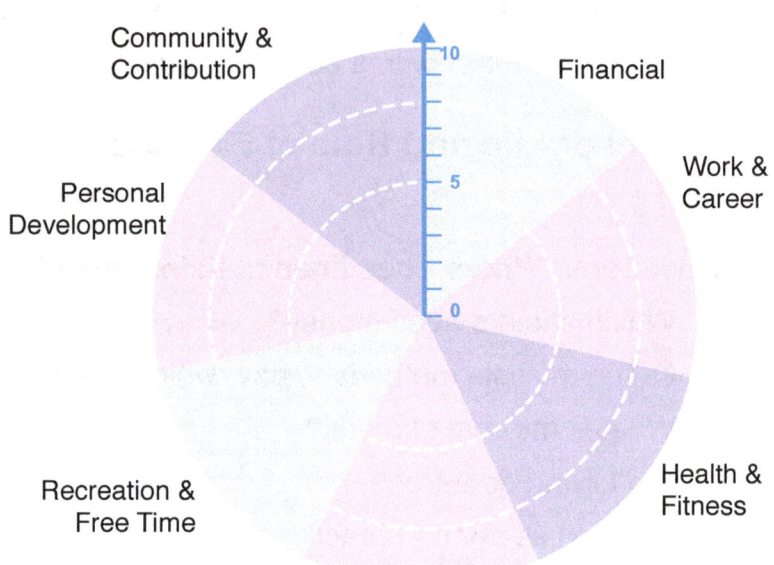

INSTRUCTIONS
To fill out your Wheel of Life, score your level of satisfaction in each of seven areas of your life. Zero being that you are not at all satisfied, and ten being that you're extremely satisfied where you're currently at.

5.2 Money IQ and EQ

There are two main categories to learning about money:

Money IQ: all about money knowledge and skills

And

Money EQ: exhibiting emotional intelligence with money

There are main 2 categories to my learning about Money:

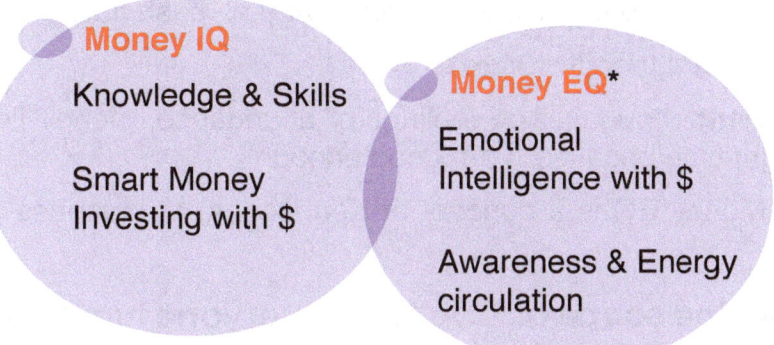

(Note: This Coaching Program focuses on Money IQ—knowledge and skills—as well as basics of Money EQ. To learn more about the latter, which we label as "Abundance Thinking", go to Chapter 11 Happiness or Conscious Wealth's advanced *eLearning Module #31*.) / *#Note: Ken Honda, Japanese money expert, suggests Money EQ is more important than Money IQ*

Let's Compare: **Money IQ vs. EQ**

Money IQ

- Associated with the stock market and technical investing—outside the attention and the scope of most average folk
- Triggers FEAR, frustrations, anger, even arrogance during market highs
- Money is SCARY—be cautious
- Money requires an advisor or broker—fear of making mistakes
- **Result**: Money IQ is filled with limiting thoughts and feelings of "not being good enough"

Money EQ

- Associated with money in the bank—security
- Yet, bank money does not make me rich…
- Wealth from multiple sources of income
- Control over my money to work smarter for me
- Money is energy: it wants to flow and move in circulation to gather more value
- Thus, let money flow in and flow out (i.e., cash flow)
- Trust in a friendly future
- **Result**: thoughts and feelings of abundance; money flows to me at the right time because "I am good enough"

Note: Money EQ is a concept of Ken Honda, a Japanese personal finance expert

5.3 Within the scope of Money IQ, everyone has six main relations with money

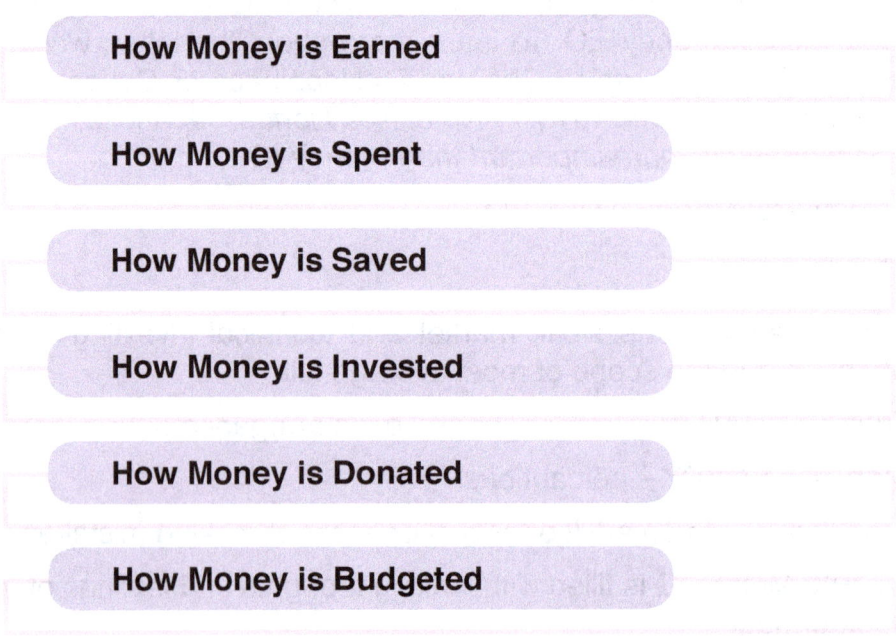

How Money is Earned

How Money is Spent

How Money is Saved

How Money is Invested

How Money is Donated

How Money is Budgeted

None of these relations is superior or vastly more important than the others. Your challenge is to endeavour towards a harmony and balance among these inter-related money relations. In terms of wealth building, it might be stated that Earning is primary function yet how money is spent or how money is invested can certainly contribute to wealthy assets also.

Conscious Wealth expands on these basics to focus attention on 8 Prime Money Functions that Form a Foundation of Financial Intelligence

Conscious Wealth's 8 Money Functions form a foundation of Basic Financial Intelligence

1. Income
2. Spend
3. Save
4. Invest
5. Donate
6. Budget
7. Dreams – Wishes

* Note the top 7 of the 8 money functions are fully explained during this program.

The 8th money function (Rewards) is highly subjective and personal. Its strongest impact occurs when goal setting (refer to Chapter 9).

Why clarity about money functions matters…

Realize that 8 Money Functions:

- Relates me to my daily basic human needs
- Reflects my orientation to money/wealth and how I think about money
- Can be a "mirror" to my values (i.e., what I actually do with money)
- Money is often a source of stress and worry—notice from where this stress originates
- Money is a measurement tool
- Money and finance are <u>not</u> a storehouse of value
- Examine what I plan to DO with money to feel happy—that is the real goal!

5.4 Added Bonus: Conventional Compared with Islamic Ideas of Finance

Although Islamic finance was first established in the 7th CE, many centuries ago, Conventional finance ideas, concepts and instruments dominate the banking marketplace these days. When studying the role of money in everyday life, it is noteworthy there are alternative mechanism – such as Islamic finance.

Here is a summary of the salient differences between Conventional and Islamic finance.

Added Bonus: Conventional vs Islamic Ideas of Finance

CONVENTIONAL IDEAS & VALUES	ISLAMIC IDEAS & VALUES
• Money has a time value- hence storehouse of Value	• Money has no intrinsic Value, not a storehouse,
• The higher the reward, the greater the risk	• Human labour, ideas, cooperation & efforts create Value that Money as yardstick can measure
• Cash flow is critical	
• Profitability & Liquidity are key	• Risk & reward open to market pricing- honors private property
• Diversification in investments reduces overall risk	• Profitability relates to negotiated terms rather than being quaranteed & increase with passage of time only
• Financial markets are efficient in pricing securities	
• Manager's and shareholders' objectives may differ- yet shareholder returns/profits take priority	• Investments incur obligations and speculative short term and short selling trading are not permissible
• Reputation & credit profile – both personal & business are paramount as good credit unlocks debt capital	• Reputation & keeping promises is critical – full accountability for character development

*Note: more on values in Chapter 8.

5.5 Top 10 Money Relationships

Everywhere in the 21st CE there are at least 36+ Money Relationships we must become familiar with as Money Partners.

Five centuries ago (16th) when mercantile banking just started in Italy there were only a handful of money relationships because:

No credit cards

No mortgage lenders

No insurance brokers

No auto dealers with car finance, etc.

However, average citizens in 2020 must "master" these money relationships that now form a large framework of modern-day services (many of which we can't seem to do without) we hire, consume or otherwise purchase. Money is central to each daily financial transaction as capitalism dominates our society.

Top 10 Money Relationships changes with maturity

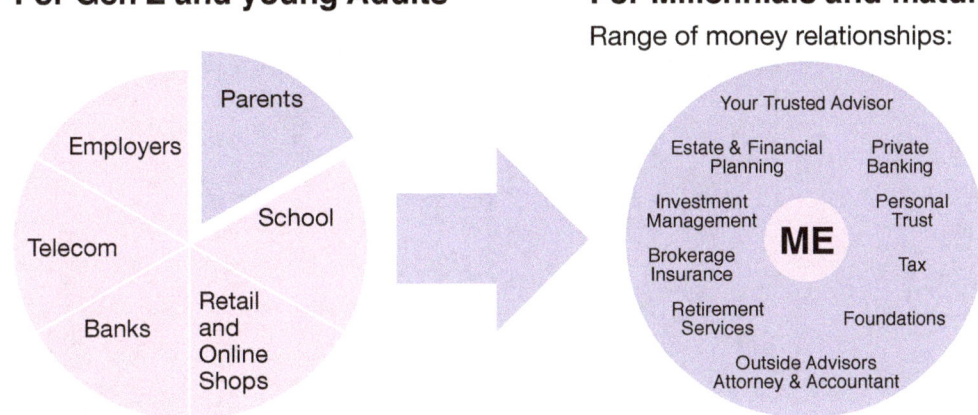

For Gen Z and young Adults

Parents, Employers, School, Telecom, Retail and Online Shops, Banks

For Millennials and mature Adults

Range of money relationships:

Your Trusted Advisor, Estate & Financial Planning, Private Banking, Investment Management, Personal Trust, Brokerage Insurance, ME, Tax, Retirement Services, Foundations, Outside Advisors Attorney & Accountant

Top 10 Money Relationships (of Top 36) based on age are fundamental to contemplate and really study to gain soild footing on your journey.

Now here are serious questions to ponder about these Money Relationships:

Q1. How do these money partners differ?

Q2. What types of resources can help you understand them?

Q3. Which require specific training or orientation?

Q4. What money partners are taught in your school?

Q5. How does each money partner operate? How do they communicate with you?

Q6. What documents or paperwork is required for each?

Q7. Do any money partners insist on a minimum age?

Q8. Which require a special contract or agreement? What is the length?

Q9. Name the money partners that adhere to Islamic finance and Shariah principles?

CONSCIOUS WEALTH

Exercise 5.2

A bank is often central to money relationships. Banks typically provide people with money, credit, business, and financial advice and act as a safeguard for savings as shown in the graphic image below:

Central to Money Relationships is a Bank. Typically, banks provide people with Money, Credit, Business and Wealth advice and act as a safe guardian for savings.

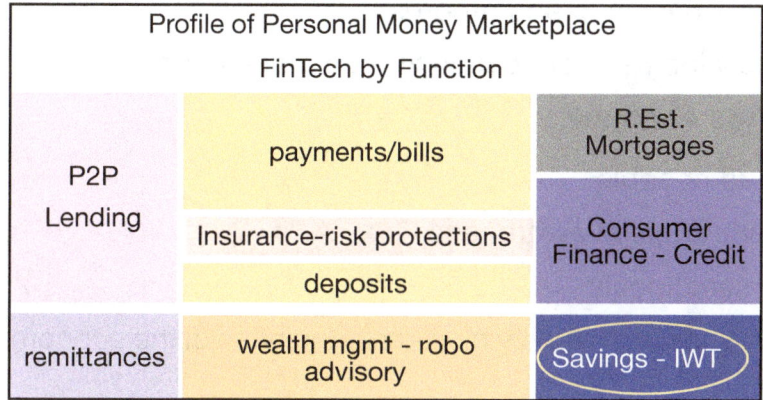

All personal wealth-building begins with SAVINGS!

Questions:

Which of these Money Relationships on left do I currently use?

Which are unfamiliar?

And which do I wish to know more about?

Which of these money relationships do I currently use?

Which are unfamiliar to me?

Which ones do I wish to know more about?

Alert: all personal wealth-building begins with SAVINGS! Therefore, set your sights on learning about various Saving tools, rates of returns and risks involved (see Chapter 12).

5.6 Purposes of Savings

Features of Savings Accounts

- Asset-building
- Instil good financial habits and financial independence
- Act as a counterweight to debts and loans
- Contribute to self-confidence
- Encourages people to look and plan ahead, setting aside resources to draw upon as new options arise and progress
- Promotes wealth-building as a foundation for national prosperity

Main Purposes of a Savings Account

- Builds assets instead of debts
- Boosts financial skills and self-awareness
- Fulfils plans for personal goals
- Expands potential for upward mobility by youth—the base of the economic pyramid for national well-being

Source: *Emerging Perspectives on Youth Savings*, CGAP-Italian Min. of Finance, 2012.

Question: What is the end goal for savings?

Answer: **Financial freedom!**

The next Diagram describes the financial freedom crossover point. Commonly measured in months or amount of monthly investment income required.

Income and expenses wall chart

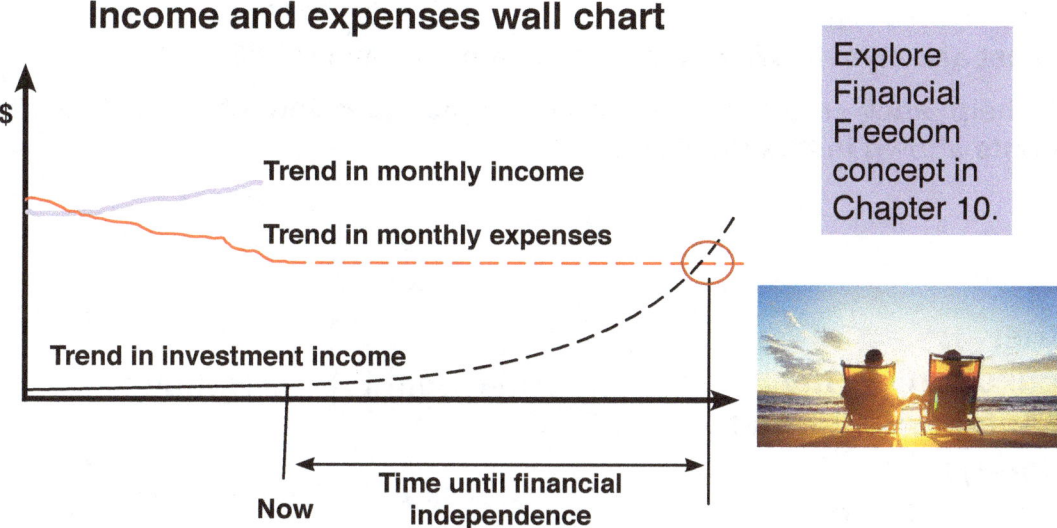

Explore Financial Freedom concept in Chapter 10.

The crossover point provides an image of financial independence. At the crossover point, monthly investment income equals monthly expenses, therefore I will be financially free. There is safe, steady income for the remainder of my life from a source (or multi-sources) other than employment for wages.

5.7 Money Moods and Money Mindset

To probe Money EQ a bit further, reflect a bit on my mental orientation to money.

I must ask myself: What is my dominant money mood?

To help answer this deceptively simple question choose 1 of the quadrants shown in this diagram:)

**After reflection On my mental orientation to Money:
Ask What is my Money Mood?**

(THEN choose 1 of these Quadrants)

Next is an explanation of the mental orientation to money represented by each quadrant.

(in Quadrants – **details**)

Explanation of mental orientation to Money

(in Quadrants- details)

C. In Control: balanced checkbook; LT financial plans; secure; "I am Enough"; extra for charity	**D. Happy:** pleasure seeking; abundance; no worries; wealth building; sets intentions & goals
A. Insecure-Anxious: uneasy about money; debt burdens; unfamiliar with finance; borrower; unable to pay all bills; needs charity	**B. Making Ends Meet:** managing finances; sometimes saver; short-term plans; feels may not deserve real wealth

This Coaching Wheel program is designed specially to provide a roadmap for me to progress from Mood A or B to Mood D. Even if my level of happiness is not sustainable day to day, I am confident, grateful for my resources and money and lessening my worries.

Yellow Flag for Caution:

A mismanagement of my Money EQ can result in my getting stuck, feelings that I struggle with money, or worse may land me in 1 or more of the 5 Money Mindset Traps.

Mindset and Money Traps to be avoided are:

- Love of money
- Scarcity of money
- Capitalism mentality and competitive mindset
- Working for money— trading time
- Owning more is better

Caution: Money Mindset Traps

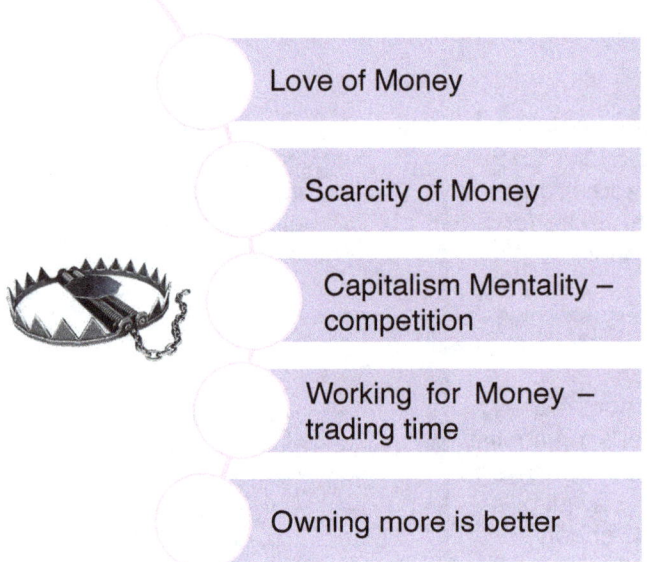

- Love of Money
- Scarcity of Money
- Capitalism Mentality – competition
- Working for Money – trading time
- Owning more is better

Hints to avoid traps

- Avoid idol worship – stirs greed
- There is abundance everywhere – scarcity is a belief on lack & limitation
- "He who have the gold makes the rules" – conquest & competitive mindset; seeks guaranteed returns
- Working only for money to buy free time & leisure (avoid this treadmill)
- Never "enough"; consuming Life & buying happiness rather than "well-being"

Brief explanation for How to Avoid Traps:

- Avoid idol worship
- Avoid scarcity thinking which is a belief of lack and limitation – never having enough attitude
- Substitute "He who has the gold makes the rules" – idea of conquest and competitive mindset and seeking guaranteed returns without risk, with collaboration and sharing of risk
- Working only for money to buy free time and leisure (avoid this treadmill)
- Unable to find joy and relax --never "enough" leads to consuming life and buying happiness rather than pursuing well-being moment to moment

5.8 Play the Empowering and Limiting Beliefs Card Game#

Exercise 5.3:

Arrange the cards by reading each and placing them into one of three columns:

(A) Yes, this is me

(B) Sometimes this is me

(C) No, this is not me

Empowering and Limiting Beliefs Game

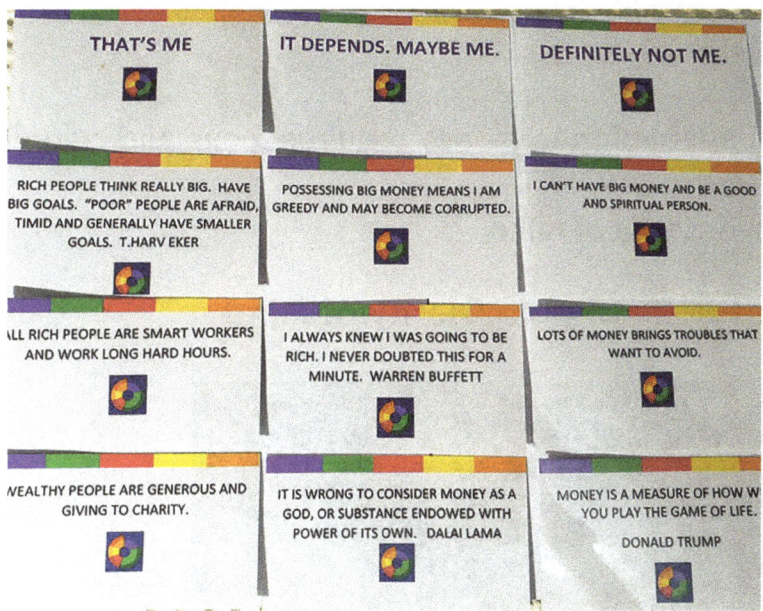

Sort the game cards into 3 columns:

1. That's Me,
2. It Depends, Maybe Me, or
3. Definitely Not Me.

Once all the cards are read and arranged as above, then reflect a few moments on those cards I put in column (A) Yes, this is me.

Did any observations or conclusions arise about your mental orientation to these Beliefs? Notice that some cards are stated as negative beliefs, while others are stated as positive beliefs.

Which beliefs do you wish to change?

#Note: Card Game is available online through www.ConsciousWealth.me

List the top 8 limitations associated with money that I believe are holding me back....

1. ....
2. ....
3. ....
4. ....
5. ....
6. ....
7. ....
8. ....

Adjusting my mental orientation to money requires focus and clarity of mind.

Here is how to achieve clarity of mind:

Develop single-point Focus to gain Clarity of Mind

Guidance to realize clarity and focus of mind:

- Single point of focus (avoid distractions and multi-tasking)
- Acknowledge that what I focus on expands and grows
- Shifting focus allows doubts and confusion to creep in and this can weaken or delay progression
- Use daily affirmations to help establish a positive state of mind
- Use detailed visualization to engage feelings/emotions and infuse emotions with the desired changes

5.9 Chapter 5 Wrap Up – High Points review

Intended Learning Outcomes:

- Identify my key relationships to money and to finance using Wheel of Life
- Understand the top 8 Money Functions and how these apply to my life
- Develop an overview of the vast range of money relationships (>36) that I must engage with as I mature
- Become aware of the 5 Money Mindset Traps to avoid
- Complete an exercise of empowering and limiting beliefs to highlight my areas of improvement and required behavioral changes

BEAUTIFUL YOU HAVE COMPLETED CHAPTER 5 AND ARE NOW AWARE OF THE MULTIPLE MONEY RELATIONSHIPS THAT IMPACT ALL AREAS OF YOUR LIFE. THIS CONCLUDES 33% OF THE ENTIRE COACHING WHEEL PROGRAM. WELL DONE!

NOW MOVING ON….THE NEXT CHAPTER IS THE NUTS AND BOLTS OF PERSONAL FINANCE, INCLUDING INCOME, BALANCE SHEETS, CASH FLOW AND NET WORTH, WHICH ARE THE BEDROCK OF INDIVIDUAL WEALTH-BUILDING AND LARGE-SCALE WEALTH-BUILDING FOR BUSINESSES AND EVEN GOVERNMENTS. LET'S CONTINUE!

conscious wealth

visit

www.consciouswealth.me

Chapter 6

Finance Tools: Balance Sheet, Income, Cash Flow

Quotes worth remembering...

"The business schools reward difficult complex behavior more than simple behavior, but simple behavior is more effective."

— **Warren Buffett**

"You can't win the game if you don't even play it."

— **Robin Sharma**

6.0 Financial Tools empowering Me to Conscious Wealth and Financial Freedom

6 Steps in My Blueprint to Conscious Wealth and Financial Freedom

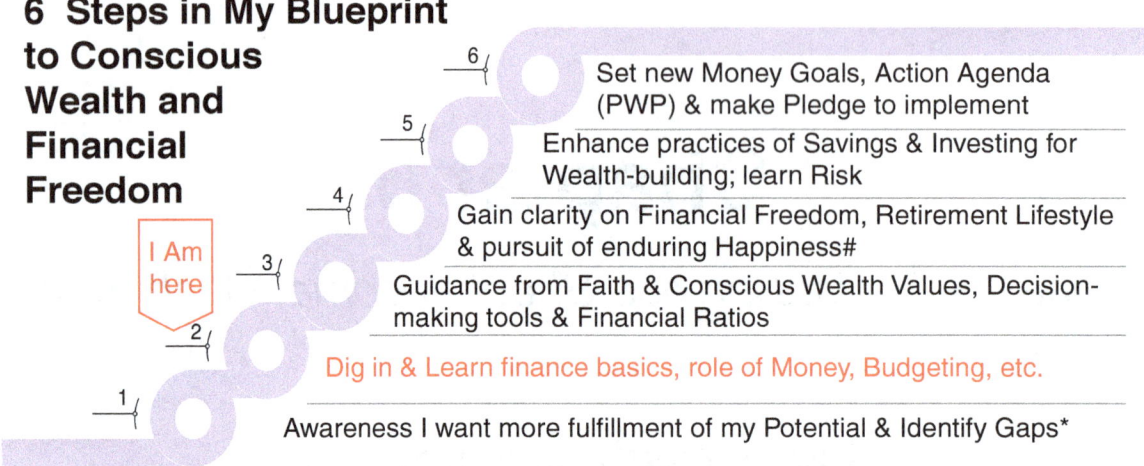

6. Set new Money Goals, Action Agenda (PWP) & make Pledge to implement
5. Enhance practices of Savings & Investing for Wealth-building; learn Risk
4. Gain clarity on Financial Freedom, Retirement Lifestyle & pursuit of enduring Happiness#
3. Guidance from Faith & Conscious Wealth Values, Decision-making tools & Financial Ratios
2. Dig in & Learn finance basics, role of Money, Budgeting, etc.
1. Awareness I want more fulfillment of my Potential & Identify Gaps*

I Am here

** Use Exercises to help find the Gaps.

#Includes Abundance Thinking which can be part of the last or first Step in this personal Journey yet essential quality to consistent, never-ending Self improvement.

What Are My Primary Outcomes of Chapter 6?

- Be familiar with cash flow statements including their purpose and how to prepare one
- Recognize what finance items are included in an income statement
- Recognize what finance items form a balance sheet and be able to calculate net worth
- Identify typical obstacles in contributing regular savings. Review tips on how to save more and which common mistakes to avoid when saving

6.1 Why Learn About Cash Flow?

A personal cash flow statement (typically one page or less) shows a person's current monthly financial condition. In short, the cash flow captures income and expenses and then compares them. There are several excellent reasons to prepare a personal cash flow statement:

- To gain control over your finances and money
- To reduce uncertainty and increase security
- Offers insight into saving money and investing wisely
- To identify and manage income and recurring expenses (often these numbers are input into a budget, see Chapter 7)
- Allows calculation of monthly net cash flow, also called "disposable income"
- Cash flow is one important measurement tool for gauging financial success

Here is a picture of Personal Cash Flow:

Is My Cash Flow Positive?

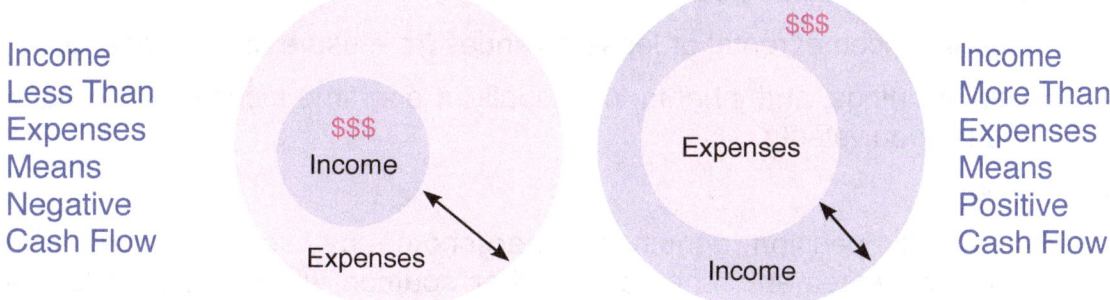

Income Less Than Expenses Means Negative Cash Flow

Income More Than Expenses Means Positive Cash Flow

Basic Equation for Net Cash Flow

Income/Gross Revenues (earnings) minus (-) **Expenses** (money spent) = **Net Cash Flow** (real financial resources available that I possess)

Take careful note, when Income is <u>Less</u> Than Expenses this means **Negative Cash Flow.**

When Income is <u>More</u> than Expenses this means Positive Cash Flow.

Basic Equation for Net Cash Flow:

Income/Gross Revenues (earnings) minus (-) **Expenses** (money spent) = **Net Cash Flow** (real financial resources that are presently available)

What are my Income cash flows?

What is my Income?

- Employment earnings/wages: wages, salary, or other compensation from employment or self-employment. Usually, periodic such as monthly or bi-weekly.
- Fee income, bonuses, and commissions: additional wages from self-employment, or fee-for-service arrangements, or annual incentive bonuses.
- Investment income: dividends or bond coupons paid out to me as the owner of securities.
- Capital gains: earnings from the sale of property, assets, or securities that is above my original cost of investment.
- Property income: rental or lease revenues from users of my property.
- Gifts, winnings, and inheritance: usually, a one-time income that is cash or cash equivalents.

<u>When retired:</u>

Social security, pension, annuity or other income: payments received from social insurance, retirement schemes or other sources which are paid to me periodically or in a lump-sum.

What are my Expenses?

- Personal living and family needs: typical monthly expenditures for food, shelter, clothing, child-care or day-care programs, bills and utilities, maintenance and repairs, entertainment, vacations, and recreation for myself and my family.

- Auto/transportation and upkeep: regular expenditures to pay for the finance of my vehicle, plus costs to maintain and operate said vehicle, or alternatively, the cost for commuting to work via public transport.

- Personal debt and credit cards: cost of repaying the purchases made on credit, as well as the interest or carrying costs associated with the temporary use of credit.

- Healthcare, medical services and other insurance: payments for insurance coverage or payments made directly for services rendered related to personal and family health and well-being.

- Education and self-improvement: fees paid for learning, tuition, books, and related training services for myself, my spouse and/or my offspring.

- Taxes: payments made to local, state (provincial) or federal (national) governmental authorities as employment tax, sales tax, property tax, income tax, or business, self-employment, or corporate tax.

- Charitable giving: money given to charitable organizations. Not strictly an "expense", but certainly an outflow of cash. (Should treat more as an "investment"—see the concept of Pious Deeds)

- Savings and investments: these items are real wealth builders, to be set aside from current cash flow now to generate more income and wealth in the future through the savings/investment vehicles I select. Not strictly an "expense", yet also an outflow of cash.

*Note: explored in detail in "Clean Wealth™ Guide to Financial Intelligence", by Dr. Omar Fisher (2021)

How to Do with Cash Flow?

Exercise 6.1: Here is a sample practice table for me to set up my monthly cash flows. Identify separately monthly income and expenses cash flows. Identify each of the following as either an "income" or "expense" item in the proper column.

Practice Cash Flows

Exercise: **Identify monthly Income and Expenses cash flows.** Identify each of the following as either "Income" or as "Expense".

Item	Income or Expense	Item	Income or Expense
Salary		Insurance Payment	
Utility Bill		Capital Gains	
Groceries		Pension	
Interest received		Rent	
Social Security Benefits		Cell Phone Bill	
Vehicle Registration		Unemployment Compensation	
Gambling Income		Tips/Gratuities received	

What can Cash Flow tell Me?

What does My Cash Flow Statement show?

- Shows my income and expenses—usually per month
- Indicates my ability to save
- Reveals my financial resources to support a standard of living
- Indicates if I am living within or beyond my means
- Highlights any financial problem areas

What is My Net Cash Flow?

There is simple arithmetic to determine my net cash flow at any point in time.

- Add up all income and earnings   +   +   +
- Subtract all expenses   -   -   -
- Equals my net cash flow   =   SR $ ¥ €

Note Three Possible Outcomes: Positive Cash Flow [I>E]; Zero Cash Flow [I=E]; or Negative Cash Flow [I<E].

My net cash flow is the second of the true starting points for developing a **Personal Wealth Plan** (PWP).

6.2 What is a Balance Sheet?

The Personal Balance Sheet tells you what you own (assets) and what you owe (liabilities). The difference between your assets and your liabilities is your net worth. Of course, the analysis between your assets and your liabilities has only three possible outcomes: a positive net worth, a zero net worth, or a negative net worth.

- **Positive Net Worth** – Assets are greater than Liabilities
- **Zero Net Worth** – Assets equal Liabilities
- **Negative Net Worth** – Assets are less than Liabilities

Naturally, if your current situation is zero or negative then you will likely encounter difficulties in beginning the Conscious Wealth management program. Rather than making investments, the next critical steps would become a systematic reduction and eventual elimination of debts, obligations, and liabilities. Only in this way can you have the on-hand resources you need to save and invest on a regular basis.

How to Prepare a Balance Sheet

Why Make a Personal Balance Sheet?

There are several good reasons to prepare a personal balance sheet. This analysis will show me (usually on one page) my current financial condition—which is the real starting point for setting future financial goals. Several reasons to draw up a

personal balance sheet include:
- To gain control over my finances and money
- To reduce uncertainty and increase security
- Major inputs to design a plan to save money and to invest wisely
- To identify and manage my assets and liabilities
- Allows calculation of net worth
- A measurement tool for gauging success

Balance Sheet Basic Equation

Assets	(things that I own)	Minus (-)
Liabilities	(things I owe others)	Equals (=)
Net Worth	(real wealth I possess)	

6.3 Elements of a Balance Sheet [please refer to Appendix template]

What are my Assets?

- Cash: checking accounts, savings accounts, money market accounts, certificates of deposit, cash value of life insurance
- Investments: shares, stocks, bonds, mutual funds, partnership interests, other investments
- Retirement Funds: pension funds, Individual Retirement Account (IRA), employee savings plans (401(k); Employee Stock Ownership Plans (ESOP), Self-Employed Plan (SEP), etc., federal social security in U.S. or GOSI (General Organization for Social Insurance- in Saudi Arabia; GPPS in UAE)
- Personal Property: Equity in home, second/rental residence, commercial property, vehicles, boats, jet planes, home furnishings, jewelry, collectibles, other assets

Some assets are wealth-creating because they generate **passive income** or increase in value over time (capital appreciation), while other assets generally decline in value (depreciate) due to usage or wear and tear (such as vehicles, home furnishings, etc.).

What are my Liabilities?

Examples of Current Liabilities:

- Charge accounts, medical bills, and credit cards
- Personal loans
- Child support or alimony (paid this year)
- Auto loans
- Investment loans (margin accounts, real estate mortgages, etc.)

Long-Term Liabilities:

- Student loans
- Home mortgages or leases
- Home equity loans
- Alimony (paid to divorcee) and child support (to be paid in future)
- Life Insurance contract loans
- Other Debts

Net Worth

Exercise 6.2

Using components of the balance sheet, personal net worth may be calculated. The formula for net worth is total assets minus (-) total liabilities = net worth.

Using the equation for net worth (above), determine my net worth. begin by listing all of my assets. Next, list all of my liabilities (refer to Chapter 2 if needed). Then using the equation, determine my financial net worth as a financial number. Of course, my net worth is much higher than this number—as is my true potential! This representation is for financial purposes only.

Net worth describes the accumulation of **wealth** in financial assets above all settled/resolved loans, debts, liabilities, and obligations.

Net worth is a measure of my true **wealth at one moment in time**, and it is one of two reference starting points for developing a **Personal Wealth Plan** (PWP). Refer back to topics covered in Chapter 2 and slide 9 herein from personal cash flow.

Just as when we begin a long journey, we prepare certain provisions, food, clothes and even money to take the trip, and it's always a good idea to take along a roadmap as well!

Only by assessing my true, present financial condition can I see where I stand and take control of the situation. I will need to do this periodically to prepare for the journey remaining towards my future financial goals and dreams.

Balance Sheet Exercise

Exercise 6.3:

What are the three financial main components that comprise my balance sheet?

- Describe some examples of assets (variable and fixed) and liabilities (short-and long-term). Which items are the biggest?
- What is personal net worth? How is it calculated?
- Why develop a personal balance sheet? Give three reasons.
- What does it tell me about my financial condition now? How can I use this knowledge in the future?

6.4 Major Threats to Savings

Even a reasonable and realistic PWP© can be derailed or blocked by threats such as:

- Lack of consistency or disciplined savings approach
- Investing "blindly" or with no apparent strategy
- High spending habits
- Early withdrawals (known as "broken trust" with myself)
- Major health problems or prolonged illness
- Disability, especially that which affects employment
- Extended unemployment without income
- Divorce
- Death of a spouse—cessation of earnings power
- Higher than budgeted education fees and expenses for children
- Unexpectedly giving financial and other assistance to aging parents in their retirement
- Severe stock market "meltdowns" or volatility resulting in sharp valuation declines. For example, Dow Jones Industrial Average in 1987 dropped 33%; in 1998 fell 15%; in 2001 declined 16% and during the Great Recession 2007-2009 fell 54% and again in March 2020 collapsed 40%.

TIPS: So, what actions shoould be avoided?

Here are some common money managing **mistakes** which are:

- Not setting measurable financial goals
- Making a financial decision without understanding its impact on other financial areas of our lives (e.g., reliance upon a broker)
- Looking for a quick fix instead of a long-term program
- Expecting unrealistic returns on investment (remember a correlation exists between risk and reward: *high reward means higher risk*)—see Chapter 9
- Believing that financial planning is only for wealthy people
- Starting strong, then losing the self-discipline to keep going

Tips to Save More

Some sound and healthy tips for increasing my savings include:

- Try to save 10% of monthly income regularly. If over 50 years of age, save 20%
- Start at an early age (between 15-22+ years). The earlier the better!
- Determine my monthly disposable cash flow (see Chapter 7 in this program)
- Pay MYSELF FIRST—set a savings amount aside every month from my income
- Contribute more savings to my special savings account whenever possible
- Review my PWP and results quarterly, and again once per year
- Be aware of inflation erosion of purchasing power—an average of 4.5% in the USA past 40 years—so try to increase my savings rate as an offset to a loss of purchasing power
- Realize that a modest 3% inflation over 35 years reduces expected retirement funds to only 40% of my plan at the age of 65 (at 85, reduction shrinks to a mere 22% of the plan)

6.5 Concluding Words to the Wise

Please keep firmly in mind that the road to wealth and riches is never smooth and straight. Every person will be tested in both wealth and poverty or suffering during life (fitnah) as described clearly in the Bible and Quran. Select references:

"As for man, when his Lord tries him by giving him honor and gifts, then he says (puffed up): 'My Lord has honored me.' But when He tries him, by straitening his means of life, he says: 'My Lord has humiliated me!' Nay! But you treat not the orphans with kindness or generosity! And urge not on the feeding of the poor! And devour inheritance - all with greed! And you love wealth with a great love!" [Surah al-Fajr V.89: 15-20]

"You shall certainly be tried and tested in your wealth and properties and in your personal selves, but if you persevere patiently and become Al Muttaqun (pious), then verily that will be a determining factor in all affairs." Al Imran V. 3:186

6.6 Chapter 6 Wrap Up – High Points review

Intended Learning Outcomes:

- Become familiar with the intricacies of cash flow statements, purposes, and how to prepare one
- Recognize the financial items that are included in an income statement and balance sheet and the purposes of each
- Know how to calculate personal net worth
- Realize the importance of savings and identify typical obstacles in making regular contributions to savings
- Review the tips to saving more and common mistakes to avoid when saving

FANTASTIC! YOU HAVE FINISHED CHAPTER 6 CONTAINING THE "NUTS AND BOLTS" OF FINANCIAL STATEMENTS. WHILE THIS MAY BE A BIT TECHNICAL, THESE FINANCIAL TOOLS ARE ESSENTIAL FOR YOU TO CONTROL YOUR MONEY AND ENHANCE SELF-CONFIDENCE IN MONEY MATTERS. SO WELL DONE!

NOW MOVING ON...THE NEXT CHAPTER COVERS BUDGETS AND HOW TO BUGET MONTHLY CASH FLOWS. THE 7X7 MAGIC BOXES CONCEPT MAKES THIS TASK EASY TO SET UP.

conscious wealth

visit

www.consciouswealth.me

Chapter 7

Budgeting

Quotes worth remembering...

"You know… you keep doing the same things and you keep getting the same result over and over again."

— **Warren Buffett**

"It's not about the end goal, it's about who you become by consistently pushing to the edge of your limits."

— **Robin Sharma**

7.0 Budgeting skills that lead to Conscious Wealth and Financial Freedom

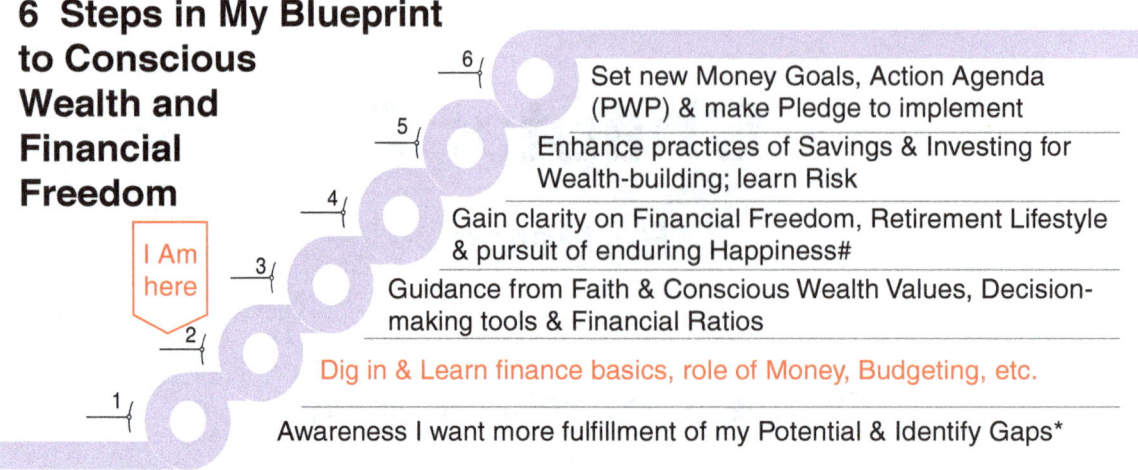

6 Steps in My Blueprint to Conscious Wealth and Financial Freedom

6. Set new Money Goals, Action Agenda (PWP) & make Pledge to implement
5. Enhance practices of Savings & Investing for Wealth-building; learn Risk
4. Gain clarity on Financial Freedom, Retirement Lifestyle & pursuit of enduring Happiness#
3. Guidance from Faith & Conscious Wealth Values, Decision-making tools & Financial Ratios
2. Dig in & Learn finance basics, role of Money, Budgeting, etc.
1. Awareness I want more fulfillment of my Potential & Identify Gaps*

(I Am here)

** Use Exercises to help find the Gaps.

#Includes Abundance Thinking which can be part of the last or first Step in this personal Journey yet essential quality to consistent, never-ending Self improvement.

What Are My Primary Outcomes of Chapter 7?

- Become aware of **sources** and **uses** of money and their differences.
- Within sources: analyze the components of which the main source is a living wage.
- Within uses: analyze the components of which the main use is living expenses.
- Examine the elements of discretionary uses and emphasize savings and investments.
- Examine the main challenges to conduct my budgeting consistently.

7.1 Sources and Uses of Money – 7x7 Magic Boxes

In any personal **capital plan,** there are both **sources** of money and **uses** of money. Note that money is <u>only one</u> type of capital: financial capital. Human capital speaks to my talents, gifts, skills, and knowledge.

> **Sources of capital**: personal income and wages, earnings, rental property income, business ownership income and dividends, royalties, winnings and prizes, gifts, inheritance.

> **Uses of capital**: personal expenses (food, home, clothes, cosmetics, personal care, hobbies, etc.), transportation (auto, trucks, buses, metro), healthcare and medical, fitness and clubs, entertainment, insurance and risk protection, education and books, subscriptions and magazines, savings, investments, charitable giving, sports and leisure, travel and holidays, retirement and pensions, etc.

> **Uses of capital**: debts and borrowings.

> **Uses of capital**: taxes and VAT

> *The first thing to notice here—number of uses of capital far exceeds sources of capital! (ways to <u>earn</u> are fewer than ways to <u>spend</u> money).*

Personal Money basics – Sources and Uses Deep Dive: Magic Boxes 7x7

Personal money basics begin with mapping out 7 Money Sources and 7 Money Uses.

Personal Money Basics – Sources and Uses Deep Dive using 7x7 Magic Boxes

7 x Sources:	7 x Uses:
1. Earned Income	1. Living Expenses
2. Rental Income	2. Debts & Loans
3. Trade – buy/sell	3. Education
4. Business Income (owner) & Dividends	4. Savings
5. Royalty – IP fees	5. Investments
6. Winnings – prizes	6. Charity - giving
7. Inheritance	7. Taxes- VAT

When personal Money Basics are described as graphic images for easy understanding, it looks like this (Step 1):

Personal Money basics

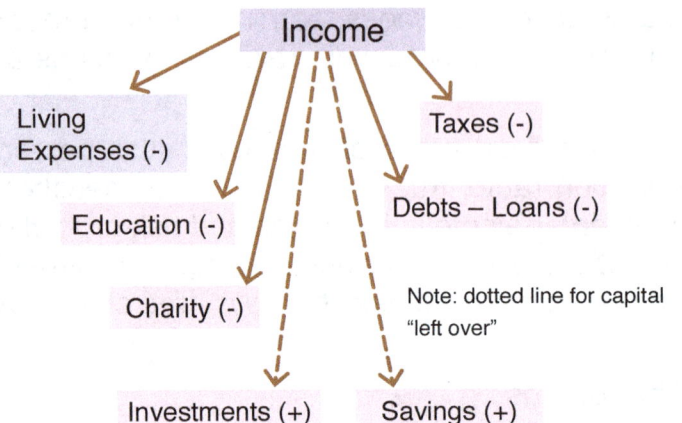

STEP #1

Uses:
1. Living Expenses
2. Debts & Loans
3. Taxes
4. Education
5. Charity
6. Savings
7. Investments

Each person's Uses for money is different. Typically, #1 Living Expenses captures the majority of available Income when spending. Other Uses are:

1. Living expenses
2. Debts and loans
3. Taxes
4. Education
5. Charity
6. Savings
7. Investments

Personal Money Basics – Tips (Step 2)

Personal Money basics

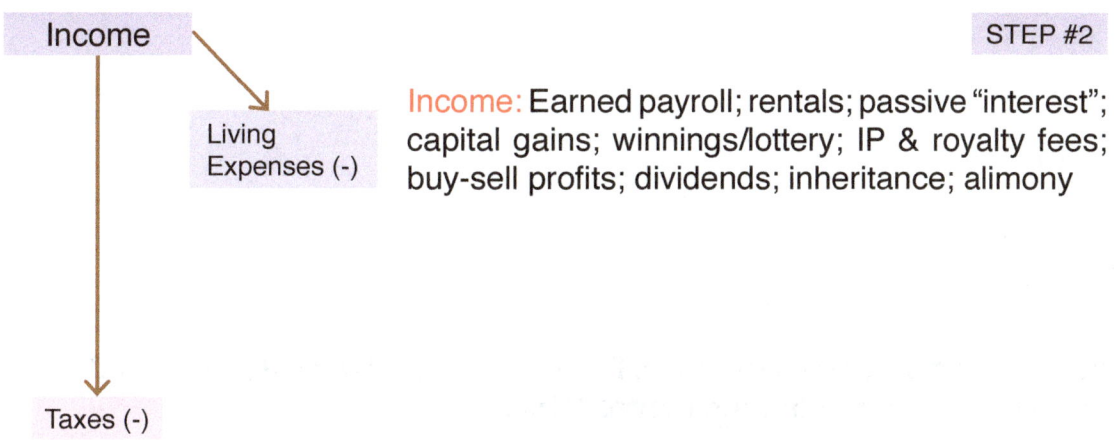

Income: Earned payroll; rentals; passive "interest"; capital gains; winnings/lottery; IP & royalty fees; buy-sell profits; dividends; inheritance; alimony

Usual types of Income are: earned payroll; rentals; passive "interest"; capital gains; winnings/lottery; IP and royalty fees; buy/sell profits; dividends; inheritance; alimony.

<u>Living expenses</u>

Living Expenses typically include food, shelter, utilities, gas, transport, vehicle repairs, travel, vacations, health and fitness, spiritual growth and pilgrimage, plus lifestyle needs and insurance expenses.

Most critical box: elastic demand—wants vs. needs; budgeting; lifestyle forecasts; **Most challenging: travel and vacations; adventures; health and fitness; spiritual growth; pilgrimage**.

Taxes: federal personal income tax; business income tax; sales tax and value-added tax; sales taxes; state tax; city tax; any special levies; knowledge tax; real estate tax; inheritance and death-estate tax; tithing annual.

Personal Money Basics – Tips (Step 3)

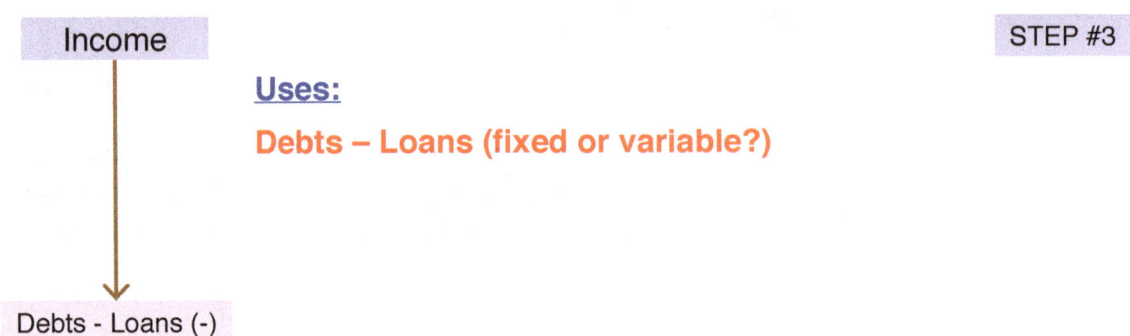

Except for emergency situations, Debts/Loans in Uses category is voluntary, and hence to a large degree controllable.

There are generally two types of Debts – fixed installments or variable installments over the agreed term of the loan.

Given the propensity for credit and loans in today's society, it is imperative that individuals assess carefully the rationale for borrowing and jts impact on the Debts already accepted to service.

Debts/Loans (fixed or variable?): personal borrowings; auto; home mortgages; second mortgages—equity line; commercial loans; line of credit and overdrafts; personal credit cards; educational loans; payday loans; pawn credit; vacation loans; employer advance payroll loans; department store credit, white goods and FFE; boat loans; recreational loans; margin on stocks and commodities; unpaid taxes liabilities

Personal Money Basics – Debts/Loans (Step 3a)

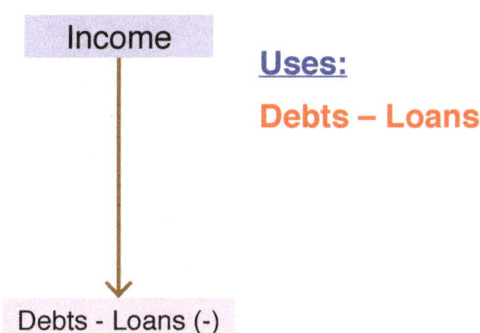

STEP #3A

There are two types of Personal Loans:
- **Secured** – with collateral or guarantee* to support the credit extended
- **Unsecured** – without collateral or guarantee backup

There are commonly two types of Debt Costs:
- **Fixed** rate of interest or profit rate (Islamic)—unchanging rate to "rent the money" usually on annual basis
- **Variable** rate of interest or profit rate (Islamic)—changing or floating rate to "rent the money"—may reset monthly, quarterly, annually (read loan terms carefully)

*Note supplying a guarantee to someone else's loan can be risky because if they default, then YOU become liable for the unpaid balance on that debt.

Personal Money Basics – Tips (Step 4)

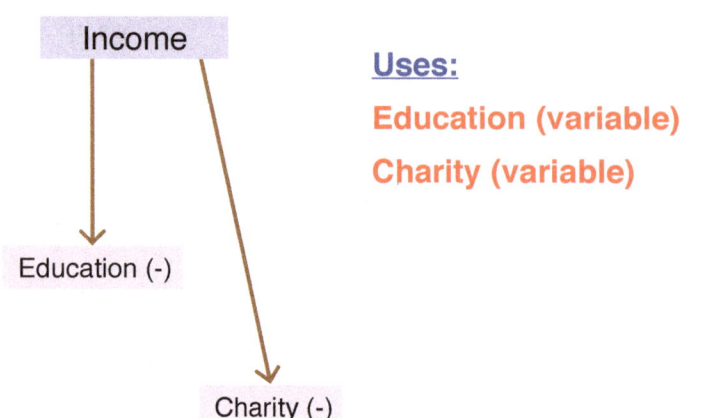

STEP #4

Uses:
Education (variable)
Charity (variable)

Other types of Uses improve individual skills or knowledge or enhance personal satisfaction by donations to a cause or charity.

Education (variable): academic learning and degrees; part-time skills; trades; subscriptions, libraries and news/film; cultural activities; books; tuition; webinars

Charity (variable): personal giving and donations; environmental gifts; foundation support; volunteerism; Corp Zakat; non-governmental organizations (NGOs); U.N. programs

Personal Money basics – Tips (Step 5)

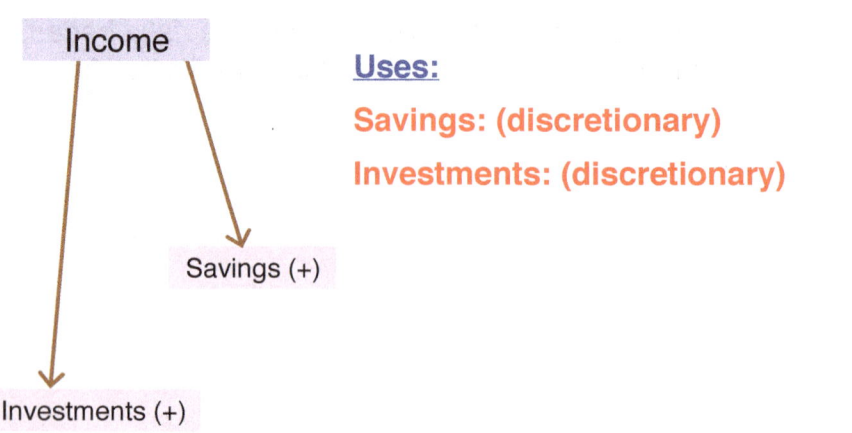

STEP #5

Uses:
Savings: (discretionary)
Investments: (discretionary)

Additional Uses may not seem like expenses but rather more like putting money aside for investing.

Savings: (discretionary) cash; Certificate of Deposit (CDs); current bank account; time deposits.

Investments: (discretionary) securities; structured finance; Exchange Traded Funds (ETFs); money market and growth funds; bonds; Sukuks; T-Bills; municipal bonds; industrial bonds and green; gold and commodities; options and futures; bitcoins; cryptocurrencies and tokens; Blockchain and smart contracts; pension and retirement assets.

Personal Money Basics – Tips (Step 6) – Subsection of Living Expenses

STEP #6

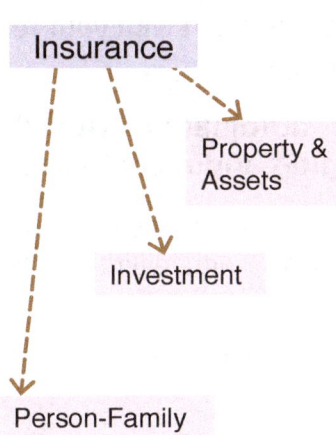

Insurance & Risk Protections:

Property & Assets: personal items; jewelry; electronics; cameras; phones; business assets; land; IP, branding;

Investments: securities; commercial real estate; lands; Private Equity & funds; Partnerships & VCs; Keyman Insurance; Gold; Crypto-currencies

Person-Family: Personal Injury & Health care; Vacations; Travel; Collectibles; LongTerm Care; Sports; Auto; Home; etc

As I accumulate property, physical and financial assets and tangible items of value, one important Uses category as expense is Insurance. Generally, there are three groupings for risk and coverage for my protection.

Insurance and Risk Protections:

Property and assets: personal items; jewelry; electronics; cameras; phones; business assets; land; IP, branding.

Investments and financial assets: securities; commercial real estate; lands; private equity and funds; partnerships and VCs; keyman Insurance; gold; cryptocurrencies

Person/Family: personal injury and health care; vacations; travel; collectibles; long-term care; sports; auto; home.

7.2 Challenges to Consistent Budgeting

Many youthful persons see a budgeting exercise as:

- Boring, unimportant and waste of time—partly because they see their income as modest
- Dull and routine
- Negative exercise—all about money limitations and restraint on spending
- Unfamiliar
- Misunderstanding of budgeting benefits

Nonetheless, the budget exercise (especially monthly) is a critical skill to develop for control over money. Moreover, budget keep you in touch with your real cashflows, and can alert to looming troubles of cash shortage.

Conscious Wealth's budgeting guidance can be automated with the MoneyPAL app#[5], which makes budgeting fun, engaging and meaningful.

7x7 Magic Boxes transforms a **budget** into a game that is an accessible, user-friendly process to make monthly money habits visible and, with a little effort, controllable.

Once the user is clear on the rules of this game, budget plans become easy and repeatable with no sweat.

Download the MoneyPAL app that can help automate monthly budgeting. Additionally, common expenses that are paid through the app are automatically tracked automatically and updated instantly to budget plans.

7.3 Why does budgeting really matter? [for budgeting template refer to Appendix]

Well, because:

- Learning to **budget** monthly cash flow can be liberating!
- A budget can be seen as a plan for spending and saving.
- A budget can connect daily habits to future success and offer full financial control.

---

5 #Note: more information online at www.consciouswealth.me

- A budget helps to establish patterns and expose spending trends.
- Budgeting efficiently puts me back in control over money (assuring me there are never more monthly days left than money!).
- A budget can be a valuable **money roadmap**.
- A **roadmap** guides me towards a destination and wards off closed streets or dead-end pathways. It can also illuminate the shortest route to my desired destination.
- Without a **money roadmap**, my journey becomes more difficult sometimes featuring unexpected twists and turns along the way.
- Without financial freedom as my destination, I might end up **NOWHERE** as any endpoint will do.
- So, I now ask myself these questions, "What is my desired financial destination? And do I have a **budget** to get there?"

7.4 Concluding Words to the Wise

"The principles always work if you work the principles!" Jack Canfield

Don't blame the past; the past is perfect as it has brought you to this moment—poised for personal transformation. Be ready to learn more!

Celebrate a new awareness; change in personal habits is never easy. Our "old, comfortable self" constantly pulls us back into that familiar comfort zone. Yet, it is always possible to break through this familiarity and find new ways of doing things.

Try on the new wings—become free and liberated from past limitations and advance towards your true self.

Remember that success takes time and perseverance. This is not necessarily hard work, but steady, forward momentum into new habits and ideals, coping with inevitable challenges, changes, and obstacles, as well as dealing with disappointment and mistakes that arise. The key is determination and practice, practice, practice.

Develop a network of support: like any journey, going at it alone is tough, so choose friends, family, relatives, and colleagues who empathize with your desire for personal change and can form a support system to assist, offer advice, encouragement, and help mobilize resources, information and solutions to resolve frustrations and quickly overcome temporary "failures".

Note: this process is not automatic. Individual results are determined by individual actions—you must do the work. However, individuals can save up to ten years by learning from and using proven models of financial learning set out by masters.

7.5 Chapter 7 Wrap Up – High Points Review

Intended Learning Outcomes:

- Awareness of sources and uses of money and their major differences
- Within sources, to analyze the components of which the main source is a living wage
- Within uses, to analyze the components of which the main use is living expenses
- Examine the budgeting process in detail as applies to me and using the 7x7 Magic Boxes system prepare a monthly personal budget
- Understand the significance of consistent budgeting and its power

AWESOME – YOU HAVE BECOME ACQAUINTED WITH BUDGETS AND COMPLETED ALL THE CHAPTERS IN STEP 2 OF THIS COACHING WHEEL PROGRAM. WELL DONE!

SO MOVING ON...STEP 3 IN CHAPTER 8 OPENS AN OPPORTUNITY TO DELIVE INTO SPIRITUAL ASPECTS AND FAITH-BASED VALUES ABOUT MONEY AND WEALTH. THE NEXT TWO CHAPTERS EXPLORE GOAL SETTING, FINANCIAL DECISION-MAKING AND WHAT CAN DEFINE PERSONAL SUCCESS. READY TO GO AHEAD?

conscious wealth

visit

www.consciouswealth.me

Chapter 8

Faith-based Values and Conscious Wealth

Quotes worth remembering...

"Someone's sitting in the shade today because someone planted a tree a long time ago."

— **Warren Buffett**

"The quality of your life is determined by the quality of your thoughts."

"Life is short. Do big things."

— **Robin Sharma**

8.0 Faith-based Values provide Guidance

6 Steps in My Blueprint to Conscious Wealth and Financial Freedom

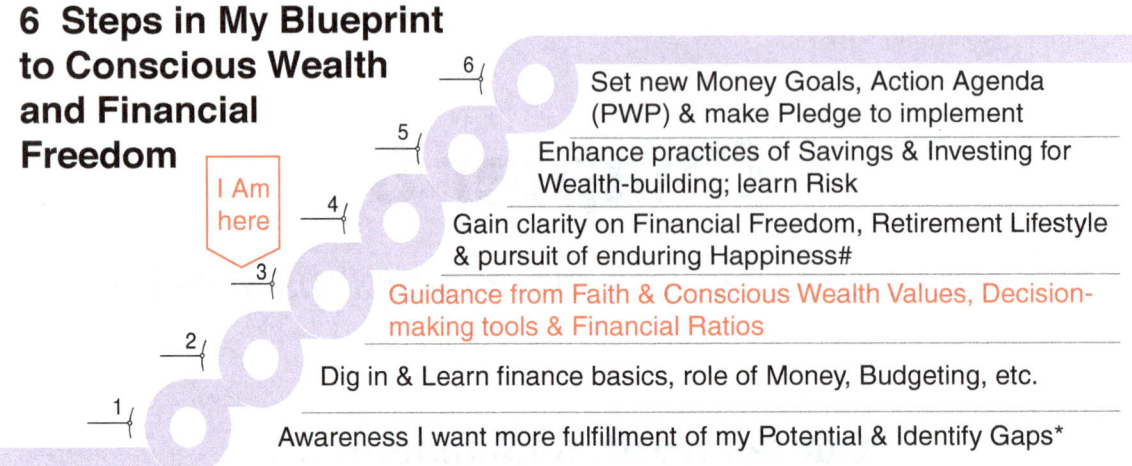

6. Set new Money Goals, Action Agenda (PWP) & make Pledge to implement
5. Enhance practices of Savings & Investing for Wealth-building; learn Risk
4. Gain clarity on Financial Freedom, Retirement Lifestyle & pursuit of enduring Happiness#
3. Guidance from Faith & Conscious Wealth Values, Decision-making tools & Financial Ratios
2. Dig in & Learn finance basics, role of Money, Budgeting, etc.
1. Awareness I want more fulfillment of my Potential & Identify Gaps*

I Am here

** Use Exercises to help find the Gaps.

#Includes Abundance Thinking which can be part of the last or first Step in this personal Journey yet essential quality to consistent, never-ending Self improvement.

What Are My Primary Outcomes of Chapter 8?

- Introduction to Maslow's Hierarchy of Human Needs and explanation of its application to financial planning
- Description of characteristics of successful, self-actualized persons and the behaviors they exhibit
- Review selected guidance from biblical sources about the role of money
- Review of selected guidance from Quranic sources about the role of money
- Familiarization with concepts in Conscious Wealth™ beginning with five ways to thrive with money for a balanced life
- Recognition that money is not wealth

8.1 One Faith-Based Outlook—Everyone is Accountable for 5 Questions

1. What did I do with my youth (up to age 16)?
2. What did I do with the body and health gifted to me?
3. What did I do with the knowledge I gained?
4. How did I acquire wealth and what did I do with that wealth?
5. What did I do with the years and life granted to me?

As a reference, cite Hadith[6]: Abu Barzah Nadlah ibn Ubayd al-Aslami narrated that the Prophet (peace be upon him) said: "A servant of Allah will remain standing on the Day of Judgment till he is questioned about his age and how he spent it; and about his knowledge and how he utilized it; about his wealth from where he acquired it and in what (activities) he spent it; and about his body as to how he used it." (Tirmidhi, Hadith 407)

What is the Purpose of My Living?

This ancient and profound question occurs to each individual at some point during a lifetime. The answer is highly personal and unique to each human being. No one else can correctly advise you about your true purpose of being alive. Each person discovers this purpose on their own and knows the irrefutable truth deep in their heart.

If you have already discovered your purpose, have embraced it with passion, and are now aligned and living that purpose daily, then you know inner peace and a sense of harmony. You confront all of life's ups and downs with self-confidence and resourcefulness.

If you are yet to uncover your true purpose, then this Coaching Wheel Program can facilitate your discovery. Abraham Maslow calls this "self-actualization". Use the various exercises throughout this program to clarify your relationship with money and finance, as well as your life purpose.

---

6 One source: https://www.alim.org/hadith/tirmidi/148

Abraham Maslow's Hierarchy of Human Needs (1943)

Maslow estimated that only one in a hundred people reach self-actualization.

Question: Are you fully living your purpose?

Everyone searches for meaning, yet self-fulfillment is a personal inner journey enabled by Abundance Thinking. Rarely is meaning found outside the person. Hence, become attuned to listening to the inner voice and identify how the paradigm (attitude) is operating that influences decisions and ways of feeling. Generally, do you enjoy positive attitude and a confident inner voice, or is that small voice in the head asserting negative thoughts, doubts and confusion?

Gaining a perspective on Self-Actualization can help re-focus on true personal success.

Abraham Maslow's Hierarchy of Human Needs (1943)

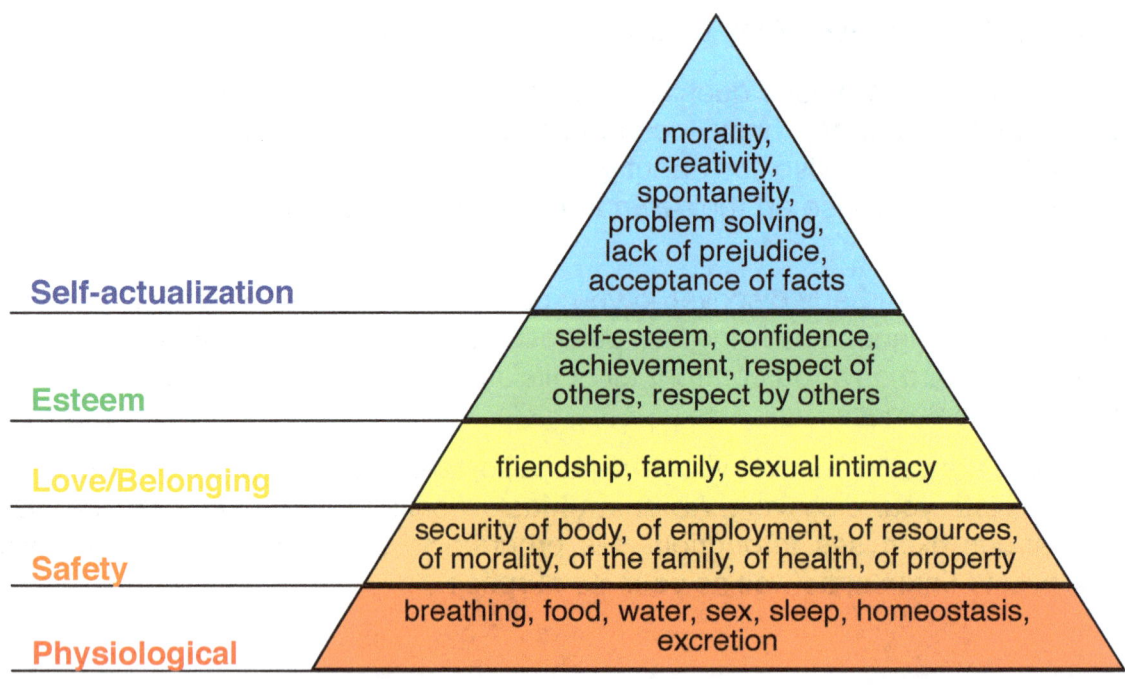

Maslow's described characteristics of a self-actualized person:
- Perceives reality objectively, factually and tolerates uncertainty
- Accepts themselves and others as they are
- Bias towards creativity, spontaneous thought, and action
- Sense of humor and light-hearted
- Compassionate for the welfare of humanity
- Capable of deep appreciation of simple life experiences
- Establishes satisfying interpersonal relationships with a few
- Orientation towards problem-solving, rather than self-centered

Question: How many of these attributes do I possess? Which ones am I working on to advance within myself?

Findings of Maslow's research (1968) on behaviors leading to self-actualization
- Experimenting with life as a child
- Trying new things instead of sticking to safe, familiar pathways
- Listening to your feelings in an evaluation of experiences, instead of the voice of tradition, authority, or the majority
- Avoiding pretense (game playing) and being authentic and honest
- Taking personal responsibility and working hard on personal goals

Maslow does not equate self-actualization with human perfection. Transcendence in mind and body forms when a person reaches their full human potential.

8.2 An Introduction to Conscious Wealth™

As part of guidance for individual self-actualization with Money, here is a description of 7 Core Principles employed daily by Conscious Wealth proponents.

Summary of Conscious Wealth™ 7 Core Principles

1. Money is not wealth. Money is energy circulating—a value promise.
2. Give attention both to how money is earned and spent.
3. Spend less than your income.
4. Plan for Financial Freedom: time and money freedoms; living debt-free
5. Wealth is the harmonious balance (well-being) of mind, body and spirit.
6. The inner state- of-being controls the outer state of reality.
7. Be grateful, give more; embrace Abundance Thinking and service to others.

Conscious Wealth innovates traditional personal financial planning by interweaving virtuous character building with wealth-building.

Money cannot buy happiness (refer to Chapter 11), and often having more money does <u>not</u> make a person more satisfied, joyful, or fulfilled in life.

Yes, this program teaches rules and tools for developing a personal financial plan as well as tips on goal setting. However, real wealth and riches become evident when an individual masters the harmonious balance of mind, body and spirit. This mastery is unique for each individual.

For this reason, Conscious Wealth's practices derive from and revolve around ancient wisdom—expressed in holy scriptures from all major religions—because these truths are revealed to man by source energy, God/Allah.

"Let there be no compulsion in religion: Truth stands out clear from Error..." (Qur'an 2:256)

Evidence from Selected Biblical Money Values

The new testament of the Bible is replete with money references. Prophet Jesus dedicated approximately a third of his teachings to money; sixteen of thirty-eight parables contained guidance on the subject of money.*

Jesus' teachings about money appear more frequently in the Bible than every other topic except the kingdom of God. Perhaps because money can become a "god" that is worshiped.*

"You cannot serve God and wealth." Matthew 6:24

"For where your treasure is, there will be your heart also." Matthew 6:21

"Command those who are rich in this present world not to be arrogant nor to put their hope in wealth, which is so uncertain, but to put their hope in God, who richly provides us with everything for our enjoyment. Command them to do good, to be rich in good deeds, and to be generous and willing to share." 1Timonthy 6:17-19

Note: * http://www.twopaths.com/faq_money.htm

Evidence from Selected Biblical Money Values

While striving for wealth and riches is certainly a worthy goal, maintain daily gratitude for whatever you may have at hand:

"But godliness with contentment is great gain. For we brought nothing into this world, and it is certain we can carry nothing out. And having food and raiment let us be therewith content." 1Timothy 6:6-8

Accumulating debts is not the same as amassing wealth (refer to Chapter 6). Moreover, debt burdens often cause dependencies and stress:

"The rich ruleth over the poor, And the borrower is servant to the lender." Proverbs 22:7

"Owe no man anything, but to love one another: for he that loveth another hath fulfilled the law." Romans 13:8

When you spend more than your income, this necessitates debts. Continuous over-spending can bring about financial weaknesses and sometimes disaster.

Evidence from Selected Quran Money Values

"Abdullah ibn Mas`ud narrated that the Prophet (peace be upon him) said, "Do not wish to be like anyone except in two cases. (The first is) A person whom Allah has given wealth and he spends it righteously; (the second is) the one whom Allah has given wisdom (the Holy Qur'an) and he acts according to it and teaches it to others." *(Bukhari, Vol. 1, Hadith 73; 255)*

"Kathir ibn Qais reported ... that Abu Darda said, I heard Allah's Messenger (peace be upon him) as saying, "Whoever follows a path in pursuit of knowledge, Allah will facilitate for him a path to Paradise. Indeed, the angels lower their wings for the seeker of knowledge … verily, the inhabitants of the heavens and the earth, even the fish in the water. ask forgiveness for Allah for the knowledgeable. The superiority of a scholar over a devout scholar is like the superiority of the moon over the stars." *(from Ibn Maajah, Vol. 1, Hadith 223[7])*

"Whoever works righteousness, man or woman, and has Faith, verily, to him will We give a new Life, a life that is good and pure and We will bestow on such their reward according to the best of their actions."   *(Qur'ân 16:97)*

Quran Answers to Money Questions

Quran answers to Key Money questions – Five to Thrive

Traditional Money Questions	Islamic Money Answers
1. How is Money earned?	• Earnings–income is Halal
2. How is Money spent?	• Spending is Halal-permissible uses
3. How is Money saved and/or invested?	• Contracts & purposes are Halal
4. How is Money donated?	• Open charitable channels: Zakat and Sadaqa
5. How is Money inherited-delivered to next generation?	• Adhere to Shariah rules for Farida (inheritance)

Selected Quran Money Values

Personal wealth-building is only a start…four <u>additional</u> money values influence a holistic and balanced approach to wealth.

Wealth Accumulation leads onto Wealth Preservation, Wealth Protection, Wealth Distribution and Wealth Purification.

---

7   One source: https://hadeethenc.com/en/browse/hadith/6267

Selected Quran Money Values

Personal Wealth-building is only a start....4 additional Money Values influence a holistic and balanced approach to wealth. Accumulation yields to purification, protection and, finally, distribution of wealth.

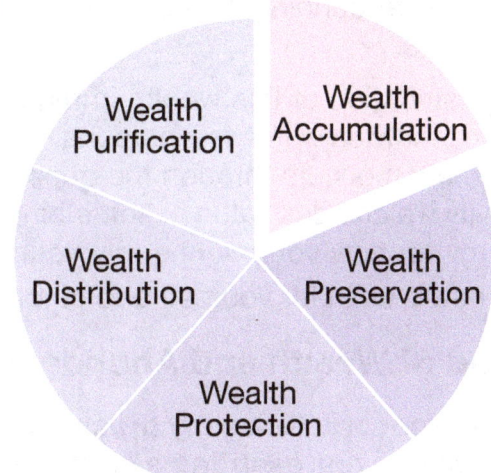

8.3 Assertion: Money is Not Wealth

Money is not the same as wealth. Money today is a fiat/paper currency issued by a central bank. The value printed on that paper is "guaranteed" as an exchange value by that bank.

At most, it is a promise only and a measurement of value created. Because we humans trust that "promise", we trade tangible goods or time and services for this paper money. Money is plentiful yet ultimately a limited supply unless more is printed*.

Wealth is everything that you desire: food, health, clean air, transportation, shelter, means to travel, clothing, jewelry, etc. Wealth can be a true feeling of abundance.

*Note * USA Federal Reserve Bank urged U.S. Treasury Mint to print 4 trillion dollars during June 2020 in efforts to reflate the economy.*

Money is a mechanism to help exchange value and to measure wealth. Most people believe that money is like a **PIE**: limited and if someone else takes a slice, there is less remaining for others to enjoy. A common worldview here is **win-lose**. For you to "WIN", then someone else must "LOSE" or another will consume your slice of pie.

Instead, re-focus on wealth, which is abundant, and a worldview of **win-win**.

Here, there is abounding wealth everywhere, so someone else's share does not diminish yours.

The distribution of this wealth in modern society may appear to be unjust or highly concentrated with a few persons. Yet, new wealth can be always be created. Wealth creation occurs through the application of human labor, knowledge, skills or creativity which adds value to something, or someone's labor. Thus, place focus and energy on how you might apply your unique talents and gifts (Chapter 2) to develop new wealth for yourself and others.

8.4 Grid of Wealth and Abundance Mindset

If I chose to caharacterize my present money mindset in one of the following four quarants – representing a continuous grid of my thinking about money and wealth, where would I place myself?

8.1 Exercise – identify where am I on this grid:

Grid of Wealth and Abundance Mindset

Exercise		
	3. Prosperity Thinking# – money is energy in circulation; sharing economy; five Senses plus spiritual	4. Abundance Thinking – focus on well-being; giving to others; feeling wealthy in all aspects
	1. Lack and Scarcity Thinking*	2. Making Ends Meet – just getting by

For fun, chose a money quadrant now and then chose again in 30 days after progressing further with this program.

Notes: *fixed supply thus belief in reductionism; take one away and the economic pie becomes smaller; hence WIN-LOSE attitude. For my WIN others have to LOSE.

#One source governs all things in the universe: energy and matter are interchangeable and all that is, hence, take one away and it transforms itself into a new form, yet the economic pie does not shrink. This attitude is WIN-WIN as my efforts to assist others to WIN makes me feel fulfilled and the pie gets enlarged.

8.5 Chapter 8 Wrap Up – High Points Review

Intended Learning Outcomes:

- Stimulate personal reflections on the purpose of my life
- Introduction to Maslow's Hierarchy of Human Needs and explain its application to financial planning
- Description of characteristics of successful, self-actualized persons and the behaviors that they exhibit
- Presentation of evidence and a review of selected sacred scriptures from Biblical and Quranic sources about money and wealth
- Description of the core concepts of Conscious Wealth™--beginning with five ways to thrive with money for a balanced life
- Recognition that money is _not_ wealth

CRUSHING IT! YOU HAVE FINISHED CHAPTER 8 BY EXPLORING THE SPIRITUAL ASPECTS OF MONEY AND FAITH-BASED REFERENCES FOR PERSONAL WELATH-BUILDING. REALIZE THAT MONEY IS NOT WEALTH MARKS THE HALF-WAY POINT IN THIS COACHING WHEEL PROGRAM. FANTASTIC!

NOW MOVING ON...THE NEXT CHAPTER REVIEWS GOAL SETTING AND FINANCIAL DECISION-MAKING TO ALLOW YOU TO HONE THESE SKILLS.

conscious wealth

visit

www.consciouswealth.me

Chapter 9

Goal Setting and Personal Financial Ratios

Quotes worth remembering...

"Price is what you pay. Value is what you get."

"Rule No. 1: Never lose money. Rule No. 2: Never forget rule No.1"

— **Warren Buffett**

"Great achievement always requires great sacrifice."

— **Robin Sharma**

6 Steps in My Blueprint to Conscious Wealth and Financial Freedom

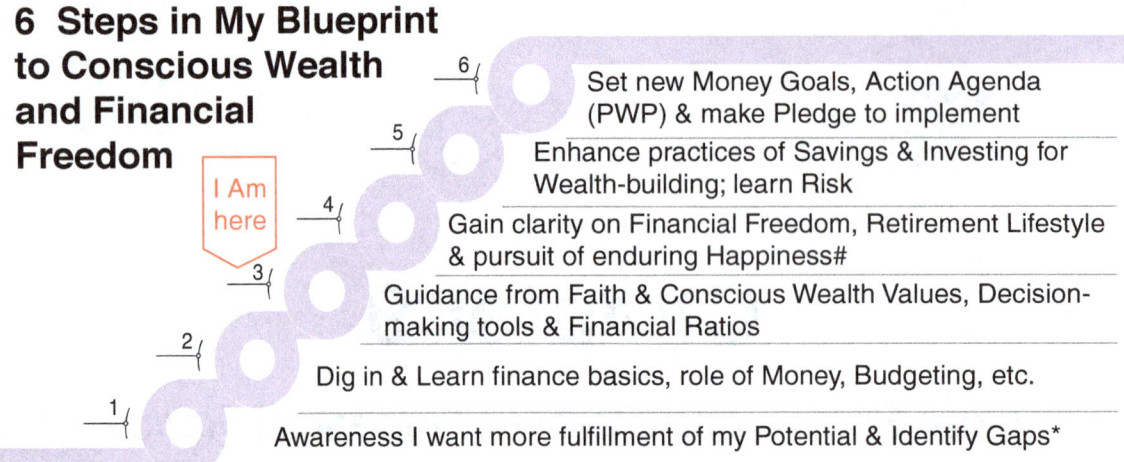

6. Set new Money Goals, Action Agenda (PWP) & make Pledge to implement
5. Enhance practices of Savings & Investing for Wealth-building; learn Risk
4. Gain clarity on Financial Freedom, Retirement Lifestyle & pursuit of enduring Happiness#
3. Guidance from Faith & Conscious Wealth Values, Decision-making tools & Financial Ratios
2. Dig in & Learn finance basics, role of Money, Budgeting, etc.
1. Awareness I want more fulfillment of my Potential & Identify Gaps*

(I Am here at step 4)

** Use Exercises to help find the Gaps.

#Includes Abundance Thinking which can be part of the last or first Step in this personal Journey yet essential quality to consistent, never-ending Self improvement.

9.0 What Are My Primary Outcomes of Chapter 9?

- Reflect on how to establish goals and why I need them
- Review *What I Really, Really Want* (Chapter 3) and transform these deep desires into a goal. Be clear on why I truly want this goal as an end, goal, not a means goal
- Prepare smart goals for my top five goals—include vision and stretch type goals
- Introduction to basic personal financial ratios
- Explanation of how to calculate these financial ratios, what they mean about my finances, and when such ratios become important in financial matters

9.1 Goal Setting

There are three categories of Goals: Doing, Having, Being.

Consciously or not, I am constantly choosing among these three types of Goals to make the priority of my actions.

There are 3 Categories of Goals:

Doing
- Doing Goal1 – what I want to plan to do in the future
- Doing Goal2 – what I want to make with hands, tools, intellect, or to achieve as degrees, certificates, diplomas

Having
- Having Goal1 – what I want to own, possess, or acquire as material objects
- Having Goal2 – what I want to be connected to as relationships, partners, in love, or fame, celebrities who are my favorite subjects

Being
- Being Goal1 – what I want to experience as in travel, adventure, specific surrounding or environment
- Being Goal2 – who I want to become, self-identity (may relate to second Having Goal)

There are three types of Goals—ones (C) I know I can achieve, ones (B) I believe I may be able to achieve, and finally ones (A) that are dream-like or "stretch" goals.

Three Types of Goals

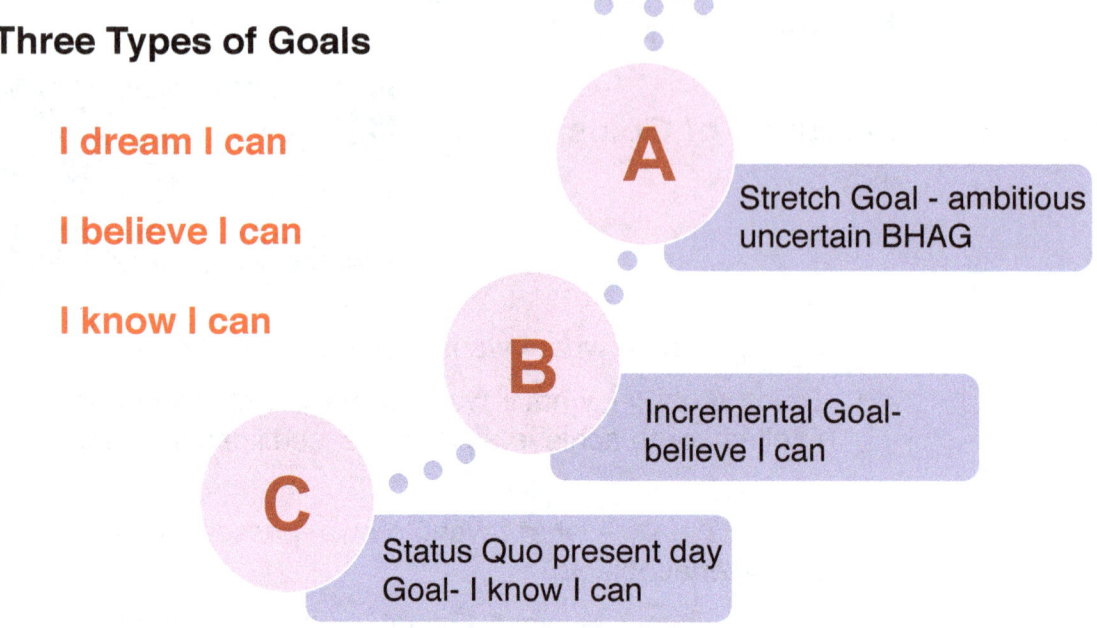

The next diagram shows the relationship between these types of goals.

Three Types of Goals

Obstacles typically arise when pursuing a B-type goal, which causes us to return to our comfort zone and perhaps get stuck with repetitive C-type goals, which results are "known" already. This result generally equals zero personal growth.

Personal growth only occurs from "Stretch" Goals, really challenging, uncertain and ambitious goals. Reach for the stars!

Three Types of Goals

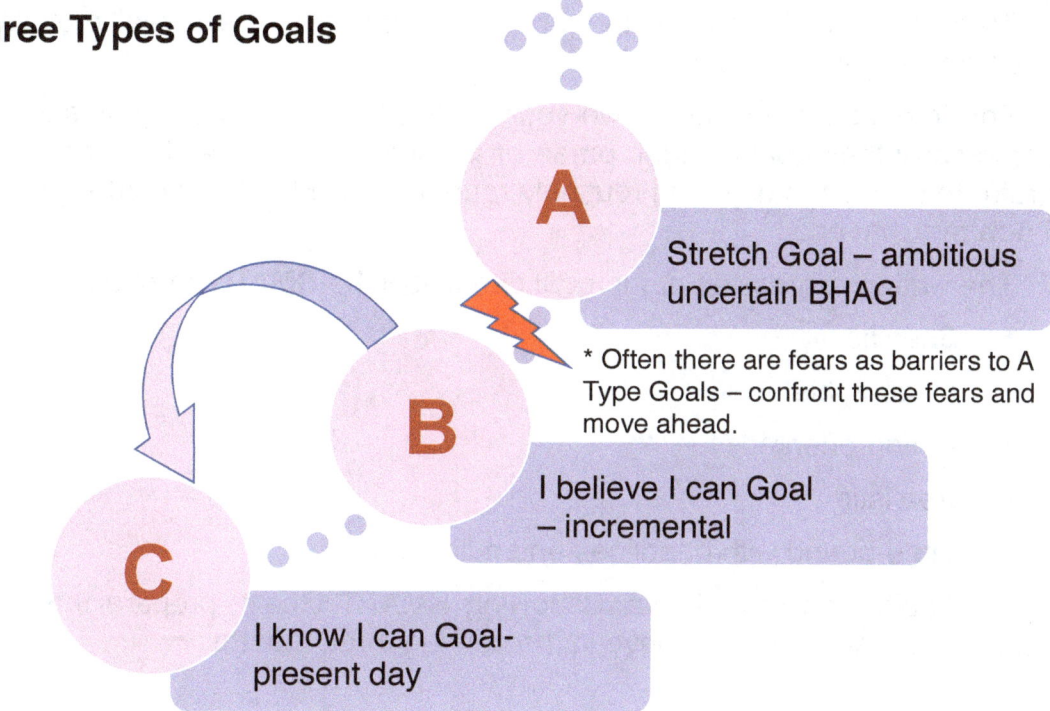

9.2 Guidance to Goal Setting – Apply SMART Goals

First rule: the goals you choose should be YOUR goals and not goals that someone else has convinced you to create. Examine your real passions, what you truly love doing, when you are engaged in these activities or services and lose track of time.

Second rule: goal(s) must be simple—few words should describe it. Easy to understand.

Third rule: goal(s) should trigger strong emotions—be a real motivator, a driver to help push you forward in life.

Fourth rule: best to write down your goal(s) to remind you (many successful people carry their goals in their purse or pockets on index cards that are handy to refer to during the day) and routinely read these and reflect on **why you want to achieve** that goal.

The written expression of the goal can follow the **SMART** formula:

- **S**pecific
- **M**easurable
- **A**ction-oriented
- **R**ealistic
- **T**ime-bound with deadlines and milestones

Now using the next diagram showing SMART Goals, prepare the top 2-4 goals you are seeking to achieve in the coming three months.

Guide to SMART Goals

Here is a template for you to use. Or you may design your own Goal Plan. It is recommended that you establish only 2-4 priority goals to be worked on during the same period.

Guide to SMART Goals

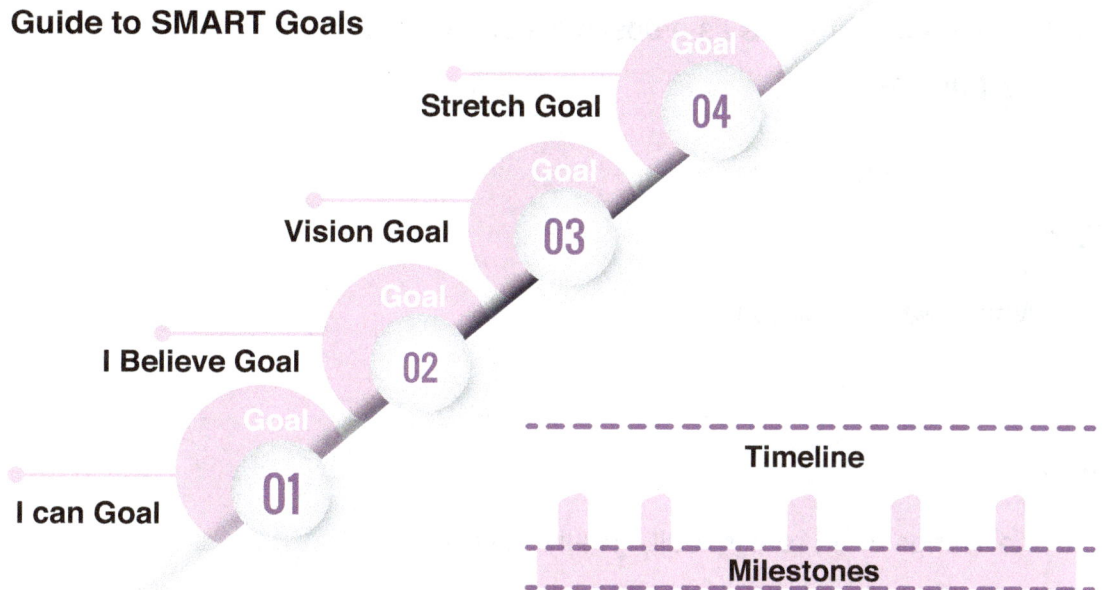

9.3 What do I really, really want?

Question: If right now I had all the money in the world, I could be located anywhere, doing anything I wanted, then I ask myself these probing questions:

"What am I doing?

Where am I?

Who am I with?

Who am I becoming?"

Use your imagination—the most powerful mental faculty and instrument we humans possess—in your mind's eye, what is the future you see for yourself?

See that new "reality" as if it is erected on a screen inside your mind. Now jump into that picture; you are now living that set of images. How does this make you FEEL? What relationships do you now have? Who is with you? Where in the world are you? What exactly are you doing?

Here there are no limitations. No judgments from others about what you should be, or any feelings of being unworthy. Here you deserve all that simply flows to you and around you.

Exercise 9.1

Write down these images as a positive statement of

1. My purpose ....
   ....
   ....

And

2. Who I want to become ....
   ....
   ....

And

3. the Things that I really, really, really desire ....
   ....
   ....

Note: add more paper if space above is not enough.

Exercise 9.2

What do I Really Really Want?

> **Exercise:**
>
> Use your Imagination…
>
> See that new "Reality" as if on a screen (inside the forehead of the Mind). Believe you are now living that set of Images. How does this make you FEEL? What relationships do you now have? Who is with you? Where in the world are you? What exactly are you doing?
>
> Here there are no limitations. Here you deserve all that simply flows to you and around you.

Clarity of Mind

Manifesting dreams into everyday reality takes clarity of mind and persistence. How to realize the required level of clarity? Here is the formula:

Clarity of Mind formula

- Single main focus
- What you focus upon expands and grows
- Shifting focus allows doubts & confusion, that weaken forward progress
- Use daily affirmations
- Use detailed visualization to engage feelings and emotions

9.4 Improve Personal Decision-Making

How Can I Improve My Decision-Making?

Apply the following decision-making guidelines to each decision I make about investments, asset allocation, and setting financial objectives.

My checklist:
- What is my time horizon? (short-term, medium-term, long-term)
- How liquid is my investment? (convert investments into instant cash)
- What are my current income needs? (age-related)
- What are my future income needs? (retirement and lifestyle-related)
- How safe is this investment? (re capital preservation)
- Does this decision allow inflation protection? (protection against loss of value)
- What is the potential for capital growth? (projected rate of increase)
- Do I have asset diversification? (asset allocation and risk mitigation)
- How do I rate the marketability? (ability to sell or convert into cash)
- Is there simplicity of management of this investment?

The factors above should be considered seriously when laying down my financial objectives.

Depending on my age, current financial circumstances, and goals, emphasis may shift among these factors. For example, younger people should emphasize capital growth and diversification, and as they approach retirement, shift to an emphasis on capital preservation and current income.

However, I should not ignore any of these important factors just because it seems like "work" to do so, as that oversight may negatively impact my accumulation of wealth and my ability to preserve my precious capital.

If the investment I prefer seems somewhat complicated, it is better to seek out a professional investment advisor for a second opinion, analysis, and assistance.

Why Having a Decision-Making Process Matters

There are several good reasons why using a Decision-Making process matters and can contribute to better results.

Most people's relationship with money is emotional. Hence, many money decisions are snap, impulsive decisions where insufficient research and preparation becomes apparent later on.

Once funds are committed, often an investment cannot be unwound or undone without penalties, fees or loss of principal capital. As the saying goes, "Think twice and jump once!"

A sound, logical checklist to aid with money decision-making establishes a process that assures higher quality financial decisions that are better aligned with stated goals.

Earnings—whether wages, passive income, or commissions—take time to accumulate as savings, which can then be transferred into investments. Thus, do not rush investment decisions. Poor, rash, or even reckless money decisions can lead to regret and significant recovery time.

Another aid available for sound decision-making includes benchmarks or financial ratios, as explained in the next subsection.

9.5 Personal Financial Ratios

Why should I know about and use personal financial ratios?

- My money habits—spending, savings, investing, donating—are all easily expressed in numbers that can be compared
- Ratios (setting relationships between select numbers) can give a picture or image to help visualize results
- Ratios make it much easier to spot trends. For example, am I getting better or worse with my money?
- Ratios enable comparison to benchmarks (common practices of others)
- Ratios quickly tell the "story" of my financial health

9.6 What do the financial ratios show me?

- The general direction of my money habits
- An outline of my personal or household financial condition
- An evaluation of how well money and financial obligations are being managed (to be judged by banks, mortgage/leasing companies, etc.)
- Quickly see where I can make changes

Ratios can be kept private, so nothing to FEAR—let's get started…

Key Personal Financial Ratios Come from three Financial Statements

There are **Hardcore Personal Ratios (6)** using Balance sheet and income statement figures, and **Advanced Personal Ratios (9)** using calculations from a balance sheet, income statement, and budget (cash flow).

Templates in the Appendix section of this program show how to prepare each of these types of financial statements. Prepare each now as inputs to the exercises that following to arrive at the personal financial ratios described next.

*Note: These are explained in Chapter 6.

Key Personal Financial Ratios come from 3 Financial Statements

HardCore Personal Ratios (6) use Balance Sheet and Income Statement figures

Advanced Personal Ratios (9) are calculations from Balance Sheet, Income Statement and Budget (cashflows)

Balance Sheet → Budget (Cash Flow) → Income Statement

Hardcore Personal Financial Ratios (6)

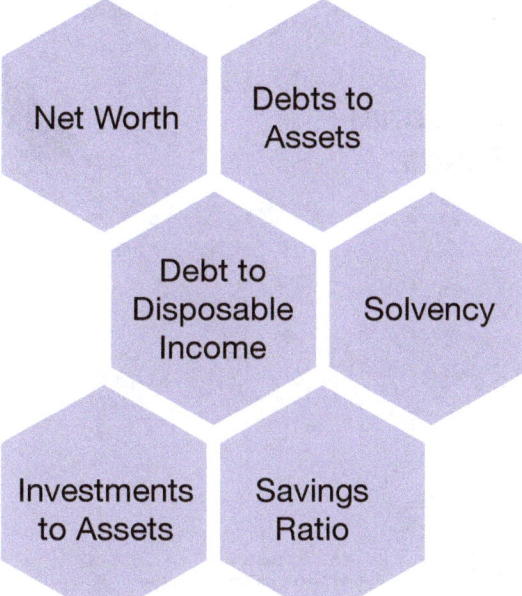

Advanced Personal Financial Ratios (9)

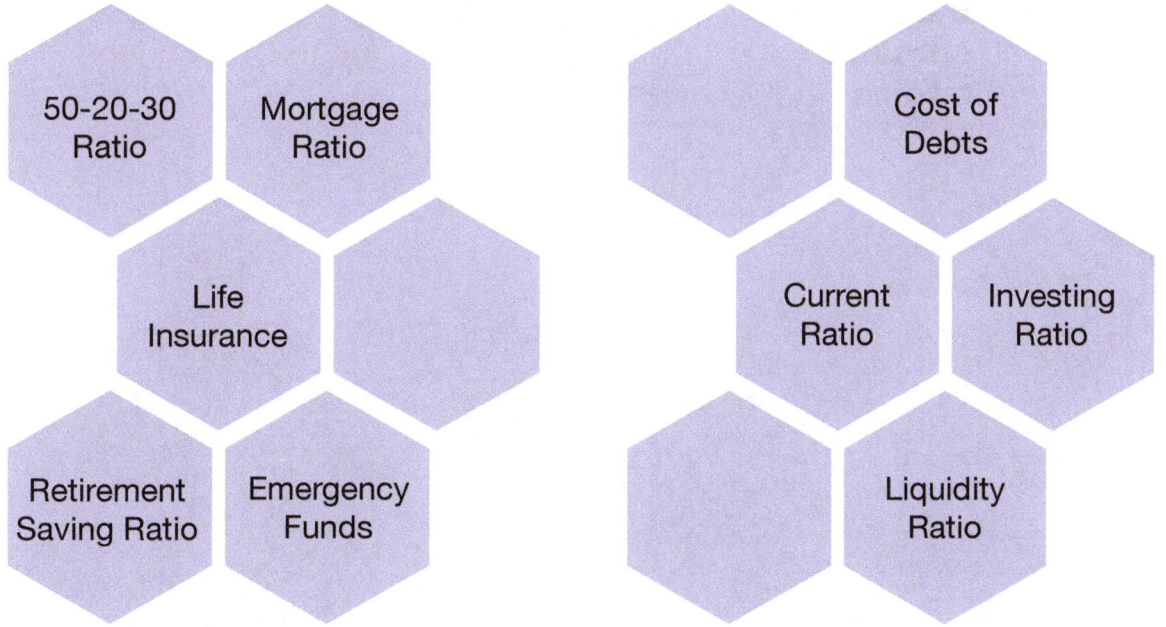

Hardcore Personal Financial Ratios

HardCore Personal Financial Ratios

Debt to Assets
- Total Liabilities/ Total Assets
- Measure of Leverage & capacity to repay Debts

→ **Balance Sheet**

Net Worth
- Total Assets less Total Liabilities
- How much "wealth you keep"

→ **Balance Sheet**

Debt to Disposable Income
- Monthly non-Mortgage debts/ monthly disposable Income
- Balance of fixed Debt outflow to discretionary Income

→ **Income Statement**

Hardcore Personal Financial Ratios

HardCore Personal Financial Ratios - 2

Solvency
- Net Worth/ Total Assets
- Inverse of leverage – of all my Assets what am I really worth?

→ **Balance Sheet**

Savings Ratio
- Yearly Savings/ Yearly Gross Income [or monthly]
- How big of a Saver are you?

→ **Income Statement**

Investments to Total Assets
- Total Investment values/ Total Assets
- Allocation of assets into LT earning securities (wealth-building for future)

→ **Balance Sheet**

Advanced Personal Financial Ratios

Advanced Personal Financial Ratios

50-20-30 Ratio
- 50% Spending; 20% Savings; 30% wants
- Eliz. Warren Guideline to consumers USA

→ **Budget/CashFlow**

Mortgage Ratio
- Monthly Mortgage Pay/ Monthly Gross Income
- Banker rule ~28% or less

→ **Income Statement**

Life Insurance
- 10X Annual Income as Face Value
- Or # months to substitute for lost Income

→ **Income Statement**

Advanced Personal Financial Ratios - 2

Advanced Personal Financial Ratios

Investing Ratio
- 120- age as % into equities with balance into bonds, real estate
- Guideline only; younger ages take more risk

→ **Budget/ CashFlow**

Retirement Saving Ratio
- Primary Yearly Income X 25 as retirement goal
- Guideline only; identify retirement lifestyle & no. of years of drawdown

→ **Balance Sheet**

Emergency Funds
- Typically 3-6 months set aside of monthly gross Income
- Cash on hand when crisis comes

→ **Income Statement**

Advanced Personal Financial Ratios

Advanced Personal Financial Ratios - 3

Cost of Debt
- Monthly Debt payments/ Total monthly Income
- Identify the average Interest-Profit Rate as price of money

→ **Budget/ CashFlow**

Current Ratio
- Short term cash/ Short term Liabilities
- Liquidity available to meet ST obligations

→ **Balance Sheet**

Liquidity Ratio
- All monetary Assets/ Monthly Expenses
- Cash & Cash-like instruments available to cover monthly Expenses

→ **Income Statement**

Why Do Financial Ratios Matter?

- Shows me the general direction of my money habits—how am I progressing?
- An evaluation of how well my money and financial obligations are being managed (as viewed by banks, mortgage/leasing companies, etc.) to be judged by such lenders when I want to borrow
- Ratios can be applied to benchmarks—either my personal ones or industry standards which are commonly accepted measurement tools
- Better that I KNOW my personal financial ratios and be in control of my finances to avoid any unpleasant surprises

9.7 Chapter 9 Wrap Up – High Points Review

Intended Learning Outcomes:

- Learn how to clearly establish goals and why we need them
- Be certain of WHY I want to achieve these stated goals—as an end, not a means, and how to prepare SMART goals
- Review of a checklist for logical and sound decision-making regarding investments
- Introduction to basic personal financial ratios and why these are important
- Realization how to calculate the main fifteen personal financial ratios and what they mean about my finances

TRUCKING RIGHT ALONG…YOU HAVE FINISHED CHAPTER 9 CONTAINING A REVIEW OF HOW TO SET GOALS, HOW TO MAKE EFFECTIVE DECISIONS, AND A DETAILED

EXPLANATION OF PERSONAL FINANCIAL RATIOS; WHAT THEY ARE; HOW TO CALCULATE THE RATIOS AND HOW THESE ARE INTERPRETED BY BANKS. GREAT WORK!

conscious wealth

visit

www.consciouswealth.me

Chapter 10

Retirement Lifestyle and Financial Freedom

Quotes worth remembering…

"It takes 20 years to build a reputation and five minutes to ruin it. If you think about that, you'll do things differently."

"If you get to my age in life and nobody thinks well of you, I don't care how big your bank account is, your life is a disaster."

— **Warren Buffett**

"Every minute spent worrying about the "way things were" is a moment stolen from creating the way things can be."

"No one will believe in you until you believe in you."

— **Robin Sharma**

10.0 Retirement and Financial Freedom

6 Steps in My Blueprint to Conscious Wealth and Financial Freedom

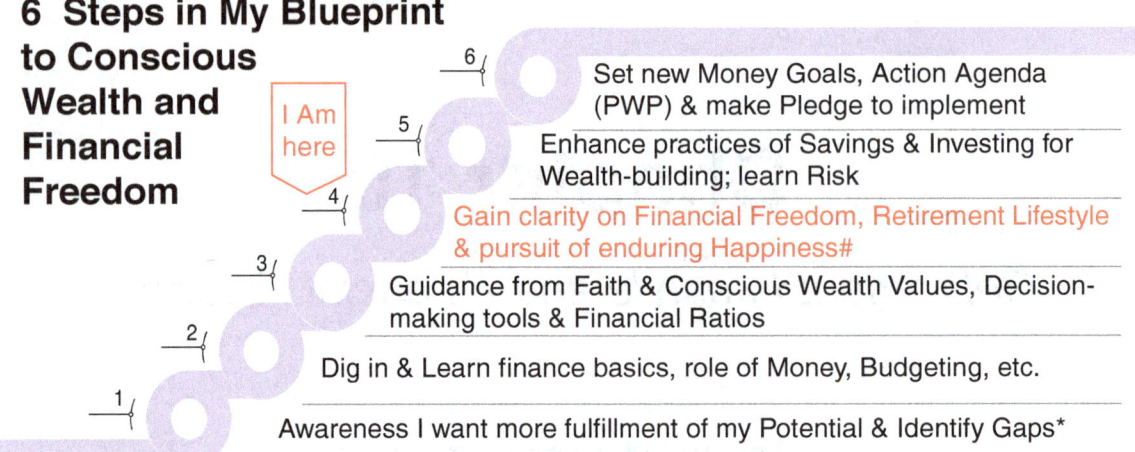

6. Set new Money Goals, Action Agenda (PWP) & make Pledge to implement
5. Enhance practices of Savings & Investing for Wealth-building; learn Risk
4. Gain clarity on Financial Freedom, Retirement Lifestyle & pursuit of enduring Happiness# *(I Am here)*
3. Guidance from Faith & Conscious Wealth Values, Decision-making tools & Financial Ratios
2. Dig in & Learn finance basics, role of Money, Budgeting, etc.
1. Awareness I want more fulfillment of my Potential & Identify Gaps*

** Use Exercises to help find the Gaps.

#Includes Abundance Thinking which can be part of the last or first Step in this personal Journey yet essential quality to consistent, never-ending Self improvement.

10.1 What Are My Primary Outcomes of Chapter 10?

- Practice visualization or imagination of the lifestyle I desire when I retire.
- Understand the concept of "financial freedom" and learn to calculate the "crossover point" for my finances.
- Understand the importance of saving for retirement—both personally and through my employer at work.
- Become familiar with retirement calculators and develop an analysis of what sum of wealth I might need to enjoy a comfortable, lengthy retirement.

10.2 Imagine Lifestyle in Retirement

Let yourself dream.

What if your bank account held as much money as you could desire?

What if you were retired and enjoyed time freedom?

Imagine a Lifestyle in Retirement

Where would you be living? Which country? Which city? Beach or mountain or suburban culture? How would you dress? How often might you travel? First Class? Tourist Class?

Which hobbies or artistic endeavors would you be doing?

Which charities are you supporting? By Money or by your time?

Use your vivid imagination to conjure images of your lifestyle in retirement, the so-called "golden years".

Imagine Lifestyle in Retirement

Exercise 10.1:

Calculate how much money is required monthly to make my retirement dreams come true.

Use my budget template (Chapter 7) as a guide to identifying the major expenditures I am likely to make each month when retired. Now multiply the monthly figure by 12 = Annual sum needed to support this desired lifestyle. ($60,000 for example)

Next, multiply the annual figure by 25 to 40 to represent the number of years I expect to enjoy in retirement (annual sum of $60,000 x 30(yrs) = $1.8 million).

So, this last figure is a goal for savings and investments to reach during my working career and lifetime of earning power (employment).

*Note: Financial means required to support a retirement lifestyle is not the same as a financial freedom crossover point (Chapter 9).

10.3 Here is the Framework to Understand Financial Freedom

Many people see wealth as living stress-free and spending time with loved ones.

When asked to put a number on what they consider wealthy, 1,000 people reported in a USA survey anywhere from $2.73 million to $3.69 million. However, less than one percent of the world's population earns more than $1 million a year.

Framework to understand Financial Freedom

So, how do I hope to join the realm of those financially free?

Framework for Financial Freedom

A working definition of financial freedom:

Financial freedom usually means having enough savings, **financial** investments, and cash-on-hand to afford the kind of life we desire for ourselves and our families during our working lifetime. It means growing savings that allow us to retire or pursue the career we want without being driven to earn a set salary each year.

Time is our most precious and non-renewable resource. Contrary to common beliefs, money cannot buy time. Money can buy comforts, tangible goods and services, and enrich leisure time. Time-space is the third dimension to describe reality. Money is the second dimension only; a numerical measurement tool made of different stuff.

One ultimate objective shared by nearly all modern humans is enjoying <u>time</u> and <u>money</u> freedoms. Source: www.moneyfit.org

Framework for Financial Freedom

Below is a diagram of financial freedom starting with the **crossover point;** commonly measured in months or amount of monthly investment income required.

Framework to understand Financial Freedom

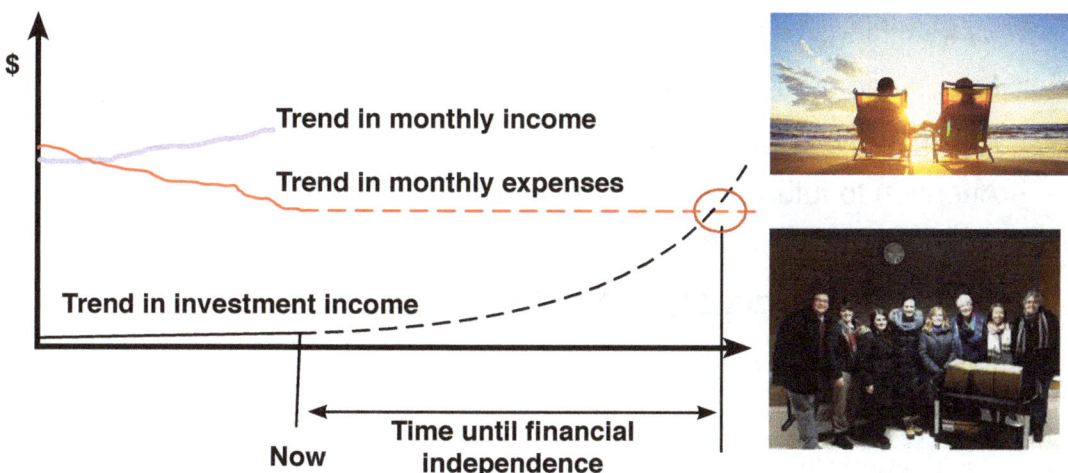

The **crossover point** provides an image of **financial independence**. At the **crossover point**, monthly investment income equals monthly expenses—hence I will become financially free. There is safe, steady income for the remainder of my life from a source (or multi-sources) other than having a job and working for wages (trading time for money).

Financial Freedom – Striking a Positive Point of View

Think about handling money with a goal of Financial Freedom in mind— there are two possible outcomes A and B.

(A) Financial freedom can feature these items

- Net worth-driven
- Goal-driven (ends)
- Pay myself first
- Concentration on Assets
- Success is sweet (desirable)
- Money to invest
- Has financial plans
- Awareness expanding
- Makes things happen
- Reads and studies (curiosity)
- Acting 100% responsible
- Attention to future (seeks solutions)

OR, using credit and heavy borrowings:

(B) Debt – credit dependency can feature these items

- Income-driven
- Work-driven (means)
- Pays others first
- Success is elusive, maybe unattainable

- Spend money
- Unclear finances (views a budget as limits)
- Concentration on Credit and Debts
- Awareness stagnant or contracting
- Things seem to "happen" to them
- Rejects reading and self-study
- Blames others
- Attention to the past (sees problems)

Financial Freedom Exercise 10.2: circle the features that currently shape your point of view, whether in column A or B

Exercise:	(A) Financial Freedom can feature these items	(B) Debt – Credit dependency can features these items
	1. Net Worth driven	1. Income driven
	2. Goal driven (Ends)	2. Work driven (Means)
	3. Pay myself first	3. Pays others first
	4. Concentration on Assets	4. Success is elusive – maybe unattainable
	5. Success is sweet – desirable	5. Spends money
	6. Money to invest	6. Unclear finances – sees budget as limits
	7. Has financial plans	7. Concentration on Credit and Debts
	8. Awareness expanding	8. Awareness stagnant or contracting
	9. Makes things "happen"	9. Things seem to "happen" to them
	10. Reads and studies – curiosity	10. Rejects reading and self-study
	11. Acting 100% Responsible	11. Blames others
	12. Attention to future – seeks solutions	12. Attention to the Past – sees problems

Note: #Adapted from Blog by Oberlo, www.oberlo.com

Financial freedom—How to Get Started

1. Make an inventory of assets and liabilities. In 2 columns note down all items (see Chapter 2)
2. Calculate your net worth (subtract total liabilities from total assets)—use this as a reference starting point (see Chapter 6)
3. Note how much cash you typically have on hand
4. Note how much cash you could raise (in an emergency) by selling/liquidating assets
5. Note the total number of loans or debts you currently have and how much of your earnings are utilized monthly to service these obligations (as a percent of gross monthly income, see Chapter 9)

These last 4 points form a basis for comparison of today vs. your future goals

** If you are happy about your findings and present situation—great!

** If you want fewer liabilities and more savings, then continue with this program study. Be confident. Say, "I CAN DO THIS". Your bright future depends on it!

Guiding Advice Along the Way to Financial Freedom

- Know your starting point (see Chapter 1)
- Set achievable, realistic goals—write these down (see Chapter 9)
- Track spending—manually on a worksheet, or via a mobile budget app
- Develop a budget (see Chapter 7)
- Try the 20-10-50-20 formula (fun living expenses; savings; ordinary living expenses; debts/loans or investments. (see Chapter 9)
- Remember: **pay yourself first** each month
- Look for ways/means to be thrifty (not stingy) and do not spend money that you don't have (meaning use credit or borrow to buy)

To boost happiness, direct some of the 20% of "fun expenses" into experiences (i.e., travel, adventures, museums, galleries, staycations, etc.) rather than buying material items. Scientific studies show (see Chapter 11) that we value experiences (and memories) more than "stuff" and these experiences contribute more to our overall happiness and personal satisfaction.

Focus your attention and efforts to pay down the debts/loans, as this will reduce stress levels and offer relief, bringing you one step closer to financial freedom.

As time and energy permits, attempt to generate additional sources of income; perform more than one sole job. This could involve a "side hustle" as a freelancer like e-commerce trading, writing, selling your photographs, etc.

Finally, remember that money is energy; it needs to circulate and is attracted where it is welcomed.

10.4 World Wealth Report 2019

Reading the pie chart shows that less than 1% of the global population makes more than $1 million annually.

According to the most recent World Wealth Report (2019), the average citizen in developed economies earns >$10,000<$100,000 annually. Whereas World Average earnings are only ~$3,000 per month.

Best guidance is to save 5-10% of your annual Disposable Income. This percent often rises with age of demographics.

Just 20% of global population is able to save more than $200,000 towards retirement. For example: Only 23% of Americans have saved more than USD50,000 for retirement, excluding the value of their home. Europe showcases a similar percentage, with average EU citizen savings less than €45.000.

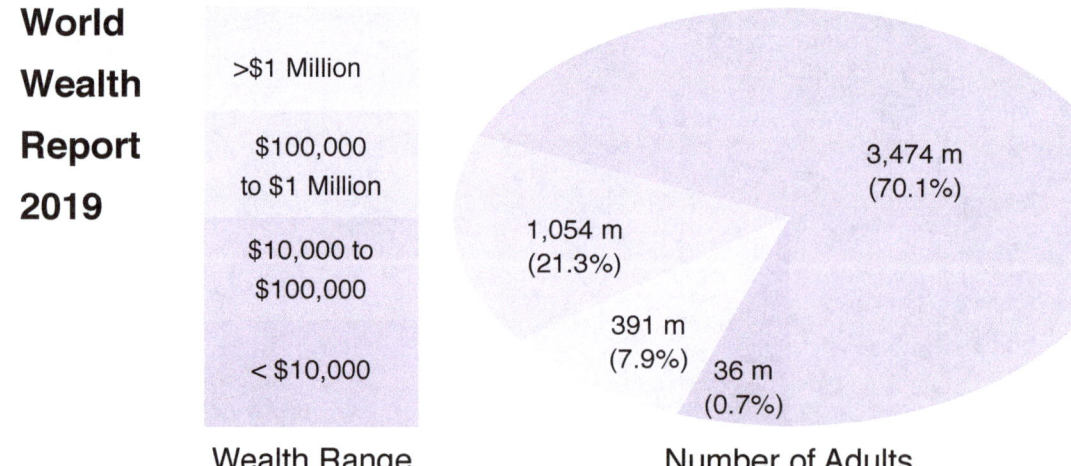

Breakdown of global wealth distribution
(U.S. Dollars)

World Wealth Report 2019

Wealth Range	Number of Adults (percent of world adults)
>$1 Million	36 m (0.7%)
$100,000 to $1 Million	391 m (7.9%)
$10,000 to $100,000	1,054 m (21.3%)
< $10,000	3,474 m (70.1%)

www.ProctorGallagherInstitute.com

Question: Which part of this graph am I in?

What Are the Benefits of Having "Enough" Money Saved?

- The World Wealth Report cites that some people today are capable of saving more than $200,000 or even millions towards retirement. So, this is possible. Tell yourself, "If they can do it, I certainly can do it!"

- At the **financial freedom** crossover point, you will possess sufficient money and free time to enjoy the things that you love to do (travel, adventure, leisure, fitness training, hobbies, sports, etc.)

- The ability and capacity to buy things when and where you choose without looking at the price tag

- Greater capacity (more money) provides additional financial resources to help others and to give to charities, associations, and other noble causes

- Pursue higher education and additional learning without student loans

- Strong savings generate a positive mental outlook that is more confident and less stressed and fearful of failures, offering the potential for greater happiness (see Chapter 12)

10.5 Meaning of Financial Freedom and Retirement Calculations

Here are some retirement realities.

Sound advice is to always take advantage of On-the-Job Retirement Plan Options such as these

Retirement Realities: Retirement Plans

Wage earner options*	Business owner options*
• Payroll deduction IRA • Roth IRA • 401(k) Plans • KEOGH Plan • Employer matching funds • Employ Stock Ownership Plans (ESOP) • Direct Investments: Mutual Funds, Stocks & Bonds • Invest Bonus-Commissions	• SEP – Self-Employed Plan • Individual Retirement Account (IRA) • Solo 401(k) • Defined Benefit plan • Re-Invest Dividends- Bonus in the business or in other investments for capital gains • Sell shareholding to Partners or Exit to Investors with cash out

*Note, the examples taken from the USA yet similar at work pension plans offered to employees or shareholders. Two main types are: defined benefit plan vs. defined contribution plan

Retirement Realities: What is Enough?

The answer to the question: "what is enough?" is subjective and can only be decided by individuals.

As a reality check, consider that:

- Average retirement monthly income from U.S. Government Social Security fund to retirees (2019) is only $1,470 monthly or about $50 per day
- Retirement age in UAE is forty-nine, ex-pats is sixty; local average pension salary is AED25,000 or $6,600 monthly
- Retirement age in Saudi is 60; average pension salary is SR 12,000 or $3,200 monthly

The retirement age in the USA was sixty-two (2013) and now sixty-six. Likewise, the age to retire is rising in UAE to sixty in ex-pats/ and forty-nine nationals, and sixty years in KSA

- To secure a generous and steady retirement income, the key is multiple sources of income: both passive and active sources that generate income for you

Start early, save often, and invest when you can to accrue and build assets towards the **financial freedom** crossover point.

10.6 Retirement realities exercise: use a calculator to figure how much should I save TODAY to retire at ease in the future.

Go to your lifestyle exercise (section 10.1). How to forecast the amount of money estimated at retirement age necessary to support my desired lifestyle?

Example: Target $1.5 m yet **gap** is $600,000; hence need to save $5,000 monthly over next five years. If the **gap** is $1.4 million, hence need to save $2,000 monthly over the next twenty-five years (aged thirty-five now). Only $537 monthly over the next forty years if aged twenty now.

Sample of retirement calculator

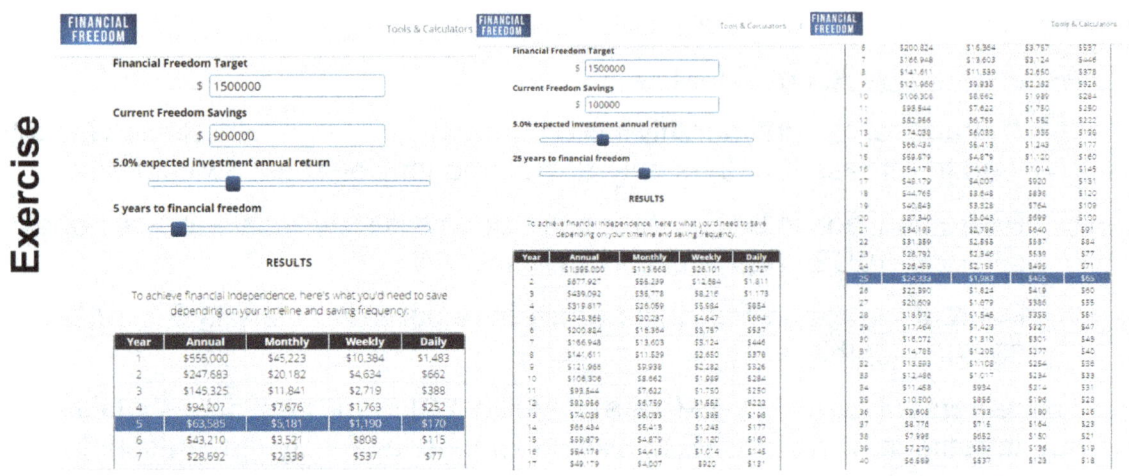

Exercise

10.2 Exercise:

1. My retirement number is = ...(in dollars/dirhams/rials)
2. What is my current savings? $ ....
3. Based upon an expected annual rate of return on savings / investment of .... percent
4. Based upon anticipated annual inflation rate of .... percent
5. Based upon the number of years remaining until retirement date = ... years

The formula is:

A. #2 X #3 X #5 = expected retirement funds; whereas I may have

B. #1 X #4 X #5 = my retirement lifestyle requirement. Hence,

C. Subtract B - A = the gap in funds.

This is the amount of annual savings/investment I must set aside to arrive at my retirement number .... (dollars/etc.)

For assistance in this calculation, refer to:

https://financialfreedombook.com/tools/how-much-money-should-you-save/

10.7 Chapter 10 Wrap Up – High Points Review

Intended Learning Outcomes:

- Conducted a visualization or imagination of the lifestyle I desire when I retire
- Understand the concept of "financial freedom" and learn to calculate the "crossover point" for my finances
- Affirm the importance of saving for retirement—both personally and through my employer at work
- Become familiar with retirement calculators and develop an analysis of what sum of wealth I might need to enjoy a comfortable, lengthy retirement

ASTONISHING – YOU HAVE COMPLETED CHAPTER 10 ON THE CALCULUS OF RETIREMENT SAVINGS BASED UPON THE IMAGINED LIFESTYLE YOU SEE FOR YOURSELF IN YOUR GOLDEN YEARS. YOU HAVE SUCCESSFULLY DONE TWO-THIRDS (66%) OF THE COACHING WHEEL PROGRAM. TIME TO CELEBRATE!

NOW MOVING ON...THE NEXT CHAPTER EXPLORES THE PURSUIT OF HAPPINESS AND HOW TO BRING HARMONY AND MORE BALANCE INTO YOUR DAILY LIFE.

conscious wealth

visit

www.consciouswealth.me

Chapter 11

Pursuit of Happiness

Quotes worth remembering...

"Basically, when you get to my age, you'll really measure your success in life by how many of the people you want to have love you actually do love you."

"It's better to hang out with people better than you. Pick out associates whose behavior is better than yours and you'll drift in that direction."

— **Warren Buffett**

"Today's a great day to behave as the person you've always wanted to be."

"Never sacrifice happiness for the sake of achievement. The real key to life is to happily achieve."

— **Robin Sharma**

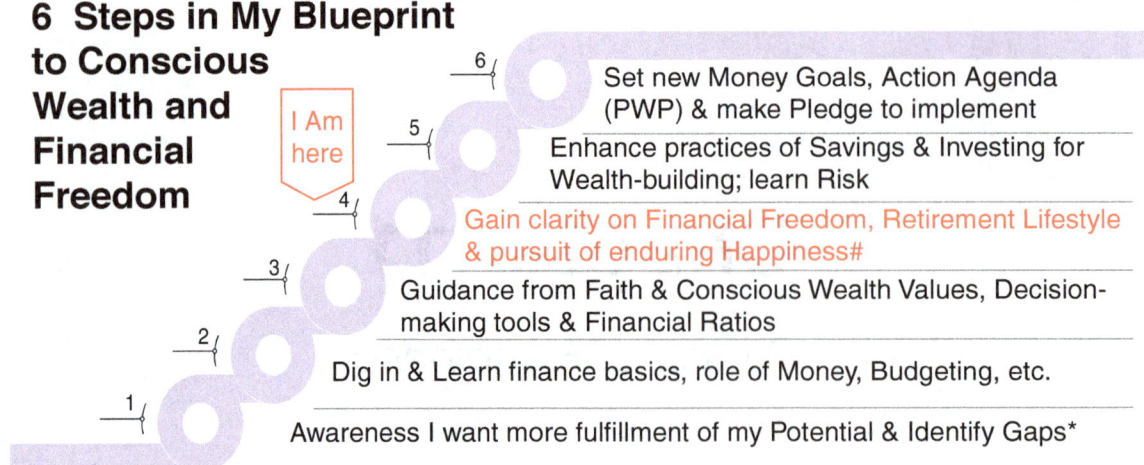

6 Steps in My Blueprint to Conscious Wealth and Financial Freedom

6 — Set new Money Goals, Action Agenda (PWP) & make Pledge to implement

5 — Enhance practices of Savings & Investing for Wealth-building; learn Risk

I Am here

4 — Gain clarity on Financial Freedom, Retirement Lifestyle & pursuit of enduring Happiness#

3 — Guidance from Faith & Conscious Wealth Values, Decision-making tools & Financial Ratios

2 — Dig in & Learn finance basics, role of Money, Budgeting, etc.

1 — Awareness I want more fulfillment of my Potential & Identify Gaps*

** Use Exercises to help find the Gaps.

#Includes Abundance Thinking which can be part of the last or first Step in this personal Journey yet essential quality to consistent, never-ending Self improvement.

11.0 What Are My Primary Outcomes of Chapter 11?

- Explore failure and success, as well as their differences
- Recognition that "failure" can be a great teacher that promotes personal growth
- Identify many so-called great persons who failed numerous times before the success that we now associate with them
- Inquiry into the science of happiness and how the human brain makes us feel happy
- Analyze the ladder of happiness and elements that contribute to sustained happiness, wholeness, and feelings of well-being
- Identify why most people struggle with money and the benefits of shifting to an abundance mindset
- Hints and tips for the art of living well

11.1 Twin Goals: Failure vs Success

No one willingly chooses "Failure"... or do they?
If I am given this choice, which option do I choose?
Which Do I Choose: Failure or Success?

Which do you Choose: Failure or Success?

- Why? What are my reasons?

- Which one is the better teacher?

While there is no correct answer, state "why" I am going with either option as those reasons are essential an awareness to informed action.

Presuming that I am a person seeking personal growth and self-knowledge, then reflect back over the past 10 years on which option has been the better **teacher**?

Main Differences Between Failure and Success

The key difference lies in attitude.

Main Differences between Failure & Success?

Failure is clear-cut, unequivocal – the results we seek and EXPECT are not achieved. We fall short, lose our assets, health, money or efforts.

Often Failure brings embarrassment, feelings of being "worthless" and fear of what others may say about us.

Success is broader, deeper with a spiritual element about how we approach Life with satisfaction.

Success is growth in personal goals and achievements.

Success is different from winning. To WIN is to be the best! Competing against others and coming out on top: better time, better score, better feats. Typically, winning is about sports, rather than personal achievement.

CONSCIOUS WEALTH

Breakdown of Failure: Having a World View

Main Differences between Failure & Success?

Positivism
- "Glass half full"
- Things will work out
- Friendly Universe

Mixed - Vacillation
- Mental shifts from Positive to Negative
- I am in charge then I am a victim

Negativism
- "Glass half empty"
- Things usually don't work out for me
- Victim outlook – why me?

Question: Which view do I usually have?

When I wake, which is the view I hold at the start of the day?

Can I sustain that view usually throughout the entire day?

Let's examine "Failure" more closely – is it always negative?

Therefore, can I conclude that: Failure is a **teacher**? or is a **destroyer**?

If I can learn to perceive "Failure" as non-success in my approach, my methods, my level of understanding, or my attitude towards the task at hand, rather than "I am that Failure", perhaps Failure can become my teacher.

Breakdown to Failure

- Is Failure a Learning Experience?
- Is Failure a nudge to adjust "unrealistic" expectations?
- Is Failure a nudge to try another method, to experiment?
- Is Failure a confirmation of what "does not work"?

Breakdown for Failure

A person does not FAIL permanently, nor become a permanent FAILURE. Only those who **QUIT** truly FAIL.

By ceasing to try, to do the work, the practice, the experiments, only then does one become a **QUITTER** and a **FAILURE**, because they have given up their dreams; falling victim to an inner belief that "I am not enough, I don't deserve to succeed…"

A **failure** is a person who settles for a lesser version of themselves—to deny their potential. Nonetheless, this choice can be temporary!

Of course, no **success** comes easily or effortlessly. It is often striving which makes the achievement all the sweeter and satisfying!

Fact: Jack Canfield was rejected over 200 times to get his book published, however, it only took one publisher to say "yes" and this led to 500 million books sold over the next 25+ years!

Success often follows "Failures"…

Source: Anna Vital, internet 2021

Observations About Success

Success certainly feels GREAT! Success feels more satisfying than failure… though it is typically just as temporary!

Once a big goal or dream is achieved, usually we set a new goal – often one that is bigger, higher, better, or more expensive. like a bigger house, faster car, more education, etc. Rarely does a person pause and reflect on how their goal was realized, what personal growth occurred, or the lessons learned through their great personal success before they move on to the next goal.

Examine your goal carefully to see if it is **incremental** (readily achievable/ nearly certain) or a **Stretch** goal—one that requires new knowledge, new skills, new striving and involves a degree of uncertainty. Only **Stretch** goals are truly worthy!

Question: **Who** do I want to **become**?

....

....

....

Note refer to Step 9 Goal Setting.

Final Thoughts on Success and Failure

Avoid aspiring to small, readily attainable dreams or goals. Choose big, audacious dreams/goals, as these are truly worthy of your efforts, energies, and dedication. These goals urge you to grow. These goals stretch and expand your paradigm#.

Some dreams may appear too large and impossible, yet these are precisely the ones that fire up the imagination, passion, and help propel us forward, even when the pathway seems difficult or filled with obstacles.

Often a big, scary goal requires a few failed attempts before it is realized, but along the way, you will discover the correct methods, roadways, and resources necessary to make it a reality.

#Note Paradigm is explained in Chapter 3 and Chapter 9.

German philosopher Geert said: "Before you can do something, first you must be something."

To fulfill a goal and gain success, we must first be attuned to the "frequency" of that success; to align our mental, emotional and physical self so that we are saying "YES" to life and the manifold challenges that stand between us and our goal.

Never allow setbacks, blockages, and naysayers to deflate your dreams or overwhelm your positive attitude and dedication to realize that success.

A focus on success takes consistent mental efforts and activity, and, at times, transforming the practice into a new HABIT. This represents a change to the paradigm*; a re-wiring of neuropathways. This can take some time. Like weeds in a garden, old habits that no longer serve us must be uprooted and removed to provide space for the potential new seeds to sprout.

Continue the focus on **WHO** you want to become! Be the success you truly desire.

11.2 Pursuit of Happiness

Question: Does money buy happiness? This is an old saying yet reflect on what is your reply today.

Where in the Human Body is Happiness?

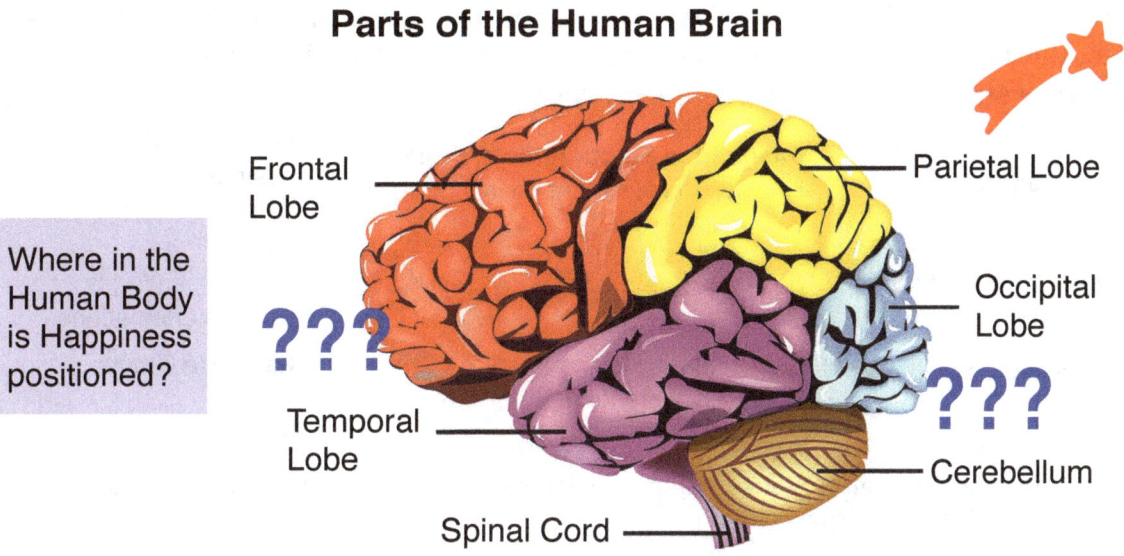

Parts of the Human Brain

Where in the Human Body is Happiness positioned?

How the Brain Processes Information

Emotions are anchored in the subconscious brain as memories, often triggered by an intense pattern of feelings due to external stimuli.

How the Brain Processes Information

Thus "happiness" feelings arrive after processing bodily Emotions, state of affairs etc. Mind record occurences, help re-create situations for happiness, and steer brain to strengthen pathways of positivity.

Autonomic	**Image/Idea Emotion/taste/smell** Unconscious-involuntary instinct	Impact on Self - image/cosmos
Somatic/voluntary	bodily conscious reaction/ Smile--**feelings**	positive affirmations
Interpretation	happiness = conscious Pleasure/contentment	hard-wire circuits

Source: Dr. Sefan Klein, IBID, p.28 Note we are more likely to avert Risk than to seek out Happiness.

Levels of happiness are associated with presence of neurotransmitters, such as:

- **Dopamine**: volition, excitement, learning, controls desire
- **Beta-Endorphin**: produced in response to pain and stress
- **Serotonin**: sends signals between nerve cells, can act as mood stabilizer
- **Oxytocin**: hormone associated with mothering and maternal love

These chemicals must be present but science is not yet fully capable of articulating <u>how</u> we humans feel. These chemicals, in conjunction with other substances, account for the creation of what human interpret as "feelings".

Also, there are pre-feelings—emotions—that first involve cerebral cortex activity. Here may exist imprints of DNA and pathways from our evolution, i.e., past lives of other humans (legacy) passed down to us. Our flight responses and fear and pleasure cues are found here, also.

11.3 Pursuit of Happiness: Common Beliefs

Two main world views or outlooks may be identified as:

A) <u>Materialism Outlook</u>: seeks external sources of happiness, achievements, and conquests, gathering material possessions to feel and be happy. However, building material wealth tends to result in an upward spiral—pushing for more and more which raises the question: "what is truly "enough"?

B) <u>Theomorphic Outlook</u>: "endearing wealth" —a range of natural experiences and man-made resources that enrich one's life and help improve character. Seeking knowledge and "knowing" god/source energy. Here, happiness feelings are connected to people, service, and contributions—centers around a purpose-driven life.

We were not designed to "destruct" and consume. Rather, we are designed to "construct"; to co-create, build, make things, and add value to what is entrusted to us.

Thus, we press forward, utilize and exploit our unique personal talents and gifts to find our passion. Dr. Wayne Dyer said: "Don't die with your music still in you."

Set some possible sample goals: **live large**. Aim for a purpose larger than yourself—a life of contribution, service, with less consumption.

Do no harm: life is cooperation, collaboration, and contentment, rather than competition and conquest; act as co-creator of the universe you want.

Focus on inner peace: know God, creator of all universes, be self-aware, cultivate healthy habits, covet resources and a fit body—which is a foundational stone of life's enjoyment, no matter how much money might be in your bank account.

11.4 Happiness vs. Satisfaction

This word distinction is important:

Happiness is what we **feel at the moment**(s) of pleasant experience(s). To feel happiness, we need elevated levels of serotonin in our brain.

Satisfaction is **what remains (images/language) in the mind**, often created in retrospect.*

The brain stores memories only at their most intense and final moments**. Thus, happiness is by nature transitory; it needs re-creation through high emotions.

*Source: Dr. Stefan Klein, Science of Happiness, p. 203; ** IBID. p. 204*

Ladder of Happiness – Dr. Moorhouse, David Nettle

There are four levels of happiness:

Ladder of Happiness

- Sensual gratification – great meal, short-lived, intense
- Ego satisfaction – being the best, smartest, most liked, competitive goals
- Love- connection – reciprocated commitment to another; person or cause; caring, loyalty; personal achievements
- Bond with higher power – God; truth; beauty; surrender to Source Energy; inner peace; passionate embrace of purpose or meaning in life

Source: Dr. Moorhouse, David Nettle

Happiness Hierarchy

The following diagram is one visualization of the levels of human happiness.

Happiness Hierarchy

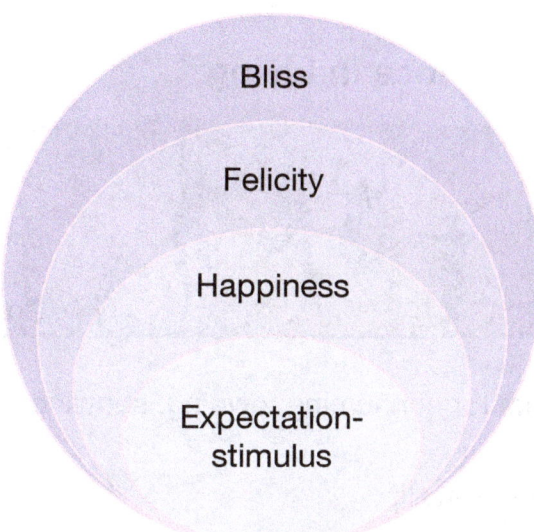

- Complete Spiritual, Mental and Bodily contentment- nirvana
- Perfect happiness, state of affairs sustained pleasure; Well Being
- Temporary "high", flush with excitement, pleasure, physical stimulus (serotonin, etc.)
- Titillation, desire, longing

Everyone experiences Titillation and Desires for things which when satisfied transforms into feelings of Happiness. Through non-attachment and practice of mindfulness, anyone can enjoy the feelings of Felicity – which occurs in a mental state of continuous happiness. Finally, when we are self-realized (often called a state of enlightenment), then those constant, steady feelings are called Bliss.

11.5 New Paradigm: Excellence in Living – Being Truly Fulfilled (Happy)

What is "authentic happiness"?

A definition is shown in the next diagram.

New Paradigm: Excellence in Living

Sustained Well-Being comes from

- Positive feelings
- Active engagement
- Uplifting connections and relations
- Alignment with positive self worth
- Choices of "ends" for their own sake, not for consuming, owning, showing off or ego satisfaction
- Not about size of wallet, bank account or payslip

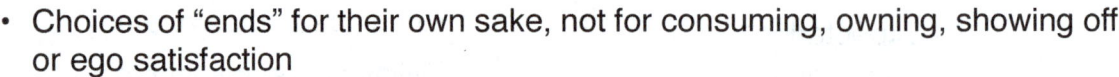

To shape our Thinking to affect the way <u>we feel</u>....intentionally use thoughts to affect emotions. *

Thus Brain plays a significant role in HOW we feel and WHAT we feel.

*Note * Dr Richard Davidson, founder of Positive Psychology UWisc USA 2012*

One Ancient Viewpoint

Many view happiness as the meaning and purpose of life; the entire aim at the end of our existence. As relates to money, is our daily focus on "well-being" or "being-well"?

One Ancient Viewpoint on Happiness

"Happiness is the meaning and the purpose of Life…the whole aim and end of human existence."

"Happiness depends upon ourselves."

"The activity of happiness must occupy an entire lifetime: for one swallow does not a Summer make."   Aristotle 3rd CE

Excellence in Living – an Abundant Life

Here are more profound quotes to ponder on an approach to sustained happiness.

"A happy life is thought to be one of excellence; now an excellent life requires exertion, and does not consist in amusement."   Aristotle

"Excellence is never an accident. It is always the result of high intention, sincere effort, and intelligent execution; it represents the wise choice of many alternatives – choice, not chance determines our destiny."   Aristotle

"Those who educate children well are more to be honored than they who produce them; for these only gave them life, those the art of living well." Aristotle

"One swallow does not make a summer, neither does one fine day; similarly one day or a brief time of happiness does not make a person entirely happy."

Source: The Nicomachean Ethics, Aristotle 356 BC CE (3rd Cen BC)

Character Traits and Talents Leading to Happiness

<u>Sages agree that happiness in life is possible through a cultivation of character traits and virtues.</u> Their starting point lies in the brain where human actions are identified as virtuous or not. These images are enhanced or diminished by accumulated experiences. Science now explains how we can re-wire the brain to nurture strength in self-identity and in desirable character traits.

Seven Cardinal Virtues or Traits are:

1. Self-Belief: having courage
2. Compassion: for self and others (leads to social justice)
3. Love and humility: are yours conditional or unconditional?
4. Patience and persistence: dedication to a goal or course of action
5. Seeking truth: comfortable with relative truth, or seeking absolute truth?
6. Wisdom: intuition and accumulated experiences
7. Moral compass: possessing a spiritual connection to a higher power, source, God/Allah—leads to a more refined consciousness

Conversely, innate talents are natural skills, aptitudes, and resources that are inherent at birth. They are often unlikely to be overhauled but may be refined through directed human efforts.

"We are what we repeatedly do." Aristotle reminds us.

Path to Well-Being – Going Beyond Happiness

One pathway to sustainable Well-Being is maintaining an attitude of detachment. To realize this outcome, try practicing these principles:

Path going beyond Happiness

1. Establish an alignment of Values with actions and deeds – a congruence; this is art of affirmative living
2. Be balanced, healthy and engaged – dynamic energies
3. Feeling abundance – from a friendly Universe
4. Make Wise choices – discovery mixed with experience
5. Have Gratitude – simplest things, even for being alive
6. Express Passion & a Purpose-driven Life – meaning is clear
7. Be grounded in Connection to Source (Taqwa), nurture Spiritual focus

This can develop into a generalized whole body and mind state of affairs which is balanced, positive, harmonious, engaged, and fulfilled (rich with meaning, purpose, and happiness). This replaces the stress, daily anxieties, worries and frustrations that many of us carry around impacting both our physical body and mind.

Well-being and Life Success Orientation – Choose a Worldview

There is a ROADMAP to **consistent happiness**.

Rich people think and view money differently than others. Most people think in terms of dichotomy—black/white; night/day; sick/healthy; either/or, etc., therefore an old paradigm controls their minds: wealthy vs. poor. However, this is "**scarcity**" thinking, conditioned by the predominant capitalist system and media world. Instead, let's open up our minds to a new mindset, a paradigm called **Abundance Thinking**.

Consider numbers zero, 1 and 2. Zero is lacking, it stands for nothing. Zero is simply a placeholder. Whereas 1 is getting started (when counting); a prime number. It is unique yes, but not as splendid as 2, which is twice as much as 1. Consider that 2 is made up of multiple aspects of 1 and is divisible by 1. So, 1 Chapter can grow into 2 Chapters. Nothing radically divergent or entirely different is required, just enrichment of 1 becomes 2. Ponder this!

11.6 Why Do We Struggle with Money?

- Money is **emotional,** a deep-seated "mirror" of our real habits and values
- Money is complicated: difficult terminology, financial engineering, cashless/ digital money, money now tied with credit (prior cash only), fiat money (paper) becomes distorted and damaged by inflation (an economic phenomenon not an asset)
- Money now is ubiquitous and central to modern activities: spending, saving, investing, insuring, charitable giving, rewarding, incentives/ bonuses, medical care, education, travel, housing, transportation, etc. Money has a 24/7 impact on our lives.
- We don't really understand happiness and try to (wrongly) use monetary tools to realize it
- Not clear on the purpose of living—**being well-off** instead of improving **well-being**

Adopt a Rich Mindset: Success Thinking

What is "Success Thinking" and how do I adopt it? Great question! Let's break this down.

How Rich people Think: A Success Mindset

- Believe that Money is Abundant and circulates
- Money comes from adding Value to others
- Ideas count more than capital...start with an Idea
- Be a Co-Creator, not a competitor
- Believe that Money/Wealth makes good deeds possible
- Take action, don't wait for Luck #
- Delve into Life-long learning, self-education and self-improvement- be positive
- Respect your precious Time: invest Time, don't waste it on too much entertainment
- Adopt Persistence - Real Wealth is earned over Time not overnight
- Leverage systems to enrich your Money/Assets, don't trade hours for wages.

Note # Luck is the confluence of preparation and opportunity, not blind destiny.

HINT: Money is an Attitude – Wave Energy Taking Form by Vibrations

A stream has only two directions: upstream and downstream Like a stream, I cannot go in both directions at once. Hence, I must choose a direction OR the prevailing stream momentum will "choose" the direction for me.

It is best to go "downstream" to be in a FLOW state and use the water current (vibration) to enhance my power when making decisions, setting plans and goals

Conscious Wealth Reminder: The 14 Success Principles for Happy Living

Taking this concept further that money is energy, I can begin to focus my attention on the thoughts that I think, the actions I am doing and the results that I see.

Success Thinking leaves traces or clues. Here is some additional guidance on how to adopt Success Thinking laid out as brief, simple principles:

1. Take 100% Responsibility
2. Be clear in what I want
3. Believe in myself and believe it is possible
4. See what I want, and get it
5. Unleash the power of goal setting (Chapter 9)
6. Release the brakes
7. "Chunk" it down
8. Take action—start now
9. Just lean into it; feel the fear and do it anyway
10. Be willing to pay the price of persistence
11. Ask questions and utilize feedback
12. Keep score and commit to constant self-improvement
13. Rule of 5—practice, practice, practice!
14. Exceed expectations—give more!

You might write each principle down on index cards with its description on the back side to help memorize them, or to remind you during the day take one card and think about how you can practice its meaning.

*Note: Adapted from Jack Canfield's 64 Success Principles, *The Success Principles* (2015). More details about these **14 Success Principles** described in Dr. Omar Fisher's eBook (2020)

11.7 Final Tips on the Art of Living Well

The art of living well, also known as well-being is knowing your passions, living with them, and enjoying them. More basic and powerful than even your thoughts.

Seek to live in ways that tap into the emotional, natural flows—happier pathways—rather than acting against them which leads to conflict, struggle, and frustration.

Three main insights can equal **wisdom**:

1. positive feelings can drive out negative ones
2. no happiness lasts forever, so seek repetition and know which moments trigger happy feelings
3. less important than <u>what</u> we experience, is <u>how</u> we experience it

Interpretation is fundamental to brain images of happiness. An active brain/body always better than a passive brain and simple observation. Dopamine reinforces activity

Activity also intensifies anticipation/expectation, which is a pre-condition to actual feelings of happiness. Stay active. Happiness comes into being passionately "busy".

*Source Note Dr. Stephan Klein, IBID p. 162

Concluding Words to the Wise

"The principles always work if you work the principles!" Jack Canfield

Don't blame the past; the past is perfect as it has brought you to this moment—poised for personal transformation. Be ready to learn more!

Celebrate a new awareness; change in personal habits is never easy. Our "old, comfortable self" constantly pulls us back into that familiar comfort zone. Yet, it is always possible to break through this familiarity and find new ways of doing things.

Try on the new wings—become free and liberated from past limitations and advance towards your true self.

Remember that success takes time and perseverance. This is not necessarily hard work, but steady, forward momentum into new habits and ideals, coping with inevitable challenges, changes, and obstacles, as well as dealing with disappointment and mistakes that arise. The key is determination and practice, practice, practice.

Develop a network of support: like any journey, going at it alone is tough, so choose friends, family, relatives, and colleagues who empathize with your desire for personal change and can form a support system to assist, offer advice, encouragement, and help mobilize resources, information and solutions to resolve frustrations and quickly overcome temporary "failures".

Note: this process is not automatic. Individual results are determined by individual actions—you must do the work. However, individuals can save up to ten years by learning from and using proven models of financial learning set out by masters.

11.8 Chapter 11 Wrap Up – High Points review

Intended Learning Outcomes:

- Explore failure and success, as well as their differences
- Recognition that "failure" can be a great teacher that promotes personal growth.
- Identify many so-called great persons who failed numerous times before the success that we now associate with them
- Inquiry into the science of happiness and how the human brain makes us feel happy
- Analyze the ladder of happiness and elements that contribute to sustained happiness, wholeness, and feelings of well-being
- Identify why most people struggle with money and the benefits of shifting to an abundance mindset

<u>Hints and tips</u> for the art of living well

- Understand the learning objectives of the financial intelligence program
- Become familiar with Conscious Wealth's pedagogy and learning approach
- Gain clarity on the benefits of this Coaching Wheel Program
- Digest an overview of the program in graphic form and become comfortable with the progression of the 6 Steps in the Coaching Wheel

- Gain awareness of the higher order-thinking and mindset insights embedded in the program

AMAZING– YOU FINISHED STEP 3 WITH AN OVERVIEW OF SCIENCE OF HAPPINESS AND GUIDANCE ON HOW TO EMBRACE MORE PERMANENT FEELINGS OF WELL-BEING. WELL DONE!

NOW SHIFTING GEARS...THE NEXT CHAPTER COVERS THE BASIC OF SAVINGS AND INVESTING. DISCOVER TOOLS, TECHNIQUES AND EXPLANATIONS ABOUT RISK AND WEALTH-BUILDING THROUGH INVESTMENTS.

conscious wealth

visit

www.consciouswealth.me

Chapter 12

Investing Basics

Quotes worth remembering...

"The stock market is designed to transfer money from the active to the patient."
"Never invest in a business you cannot understand."

— **Warren Buffett**

"When we stop taking risks, we stop living life."

— **Robin Sharma**

6 Steps in My Blueprint to Conscious Wealth and Financial Freedom

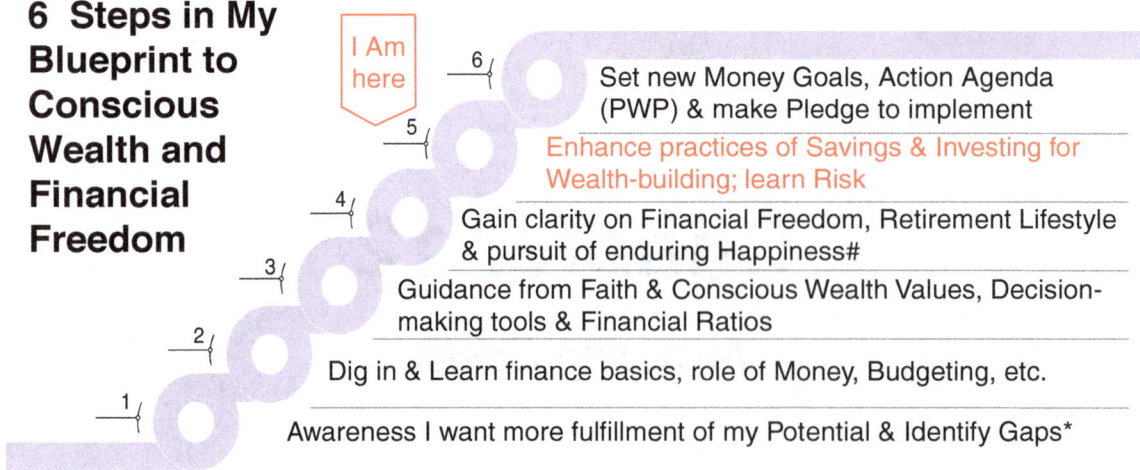

- 6 — Set new Money Goals, Action Agenda (PWP) & make Pledge to implement *(I Am here)*
- 5 — Enhance practices of Savings & Investing for Wealth-building; learn Risk
- 4 — Gain clarity on Financial Freedom, Retirement Lifestyle & pursuit of enduring Happiness#
- 3 — Guidance from Faith & Conscious Wealth Values, Decision-making tools & Financial Ratios
- 2 — Dig in & Learn finance basics, role of Money, Budgeting, etc.
- 1 — Awareness I want more fulfillment of my Potential & Identify Gaps*

** Use Exercises to help find the Gaps.

#Includes Abundance Thinking which can be part of the last or first Step in this personal Journey yet essential quality to consistent, never-ending Self improvement.

12.0 What Are My Primary Outcomes of Chapter 12?

- Become familiar with the three ways to build real wealth
- Understand the difference between savings and investments
- Describe the various types of savings options and basic rules to consider when building personal savings
- Describe the various types of Investment options and basic rules to consider when building personal investments
- Clarify what is meant by risk and return and distinguish between low-risk and high-risk types of investments
- Complete an exercise to make an asset allocation template for your investment portfolio based on your personal risk tolerances

12.1 3 Ways to Build Real Wealth

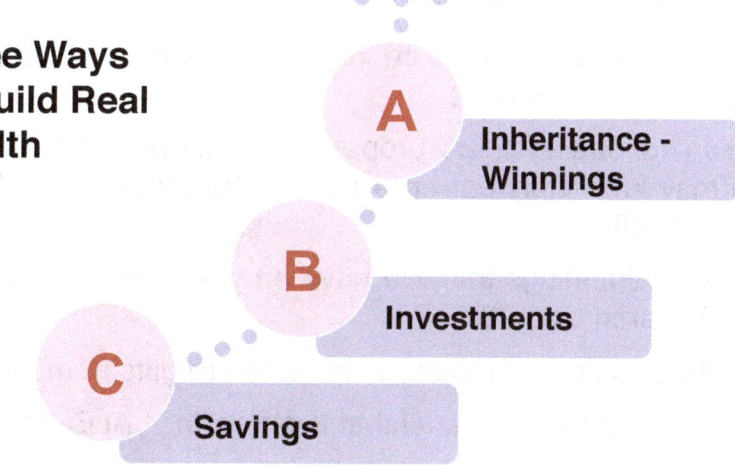

3 Ways to Build Real Wealth

1. Inheritance-Winnings: Not usually within our control. Hence, **value** is not dependable; often happenstance.
2. Investments: Self-directed yet affected by risk and asset class volatility. **Value** depends upon rates of return.
3. Savings: Self-directed with an aim for capital preservation, emergency funds, and future pension/retirement. **Value** dependent on a savings rate.

Three Ways to Build Real Wealth

A. Luck and happenstance.
B. Self-directed yet bears risk.
C. Self-directed with aim for capital preservation; can be deferred spending..

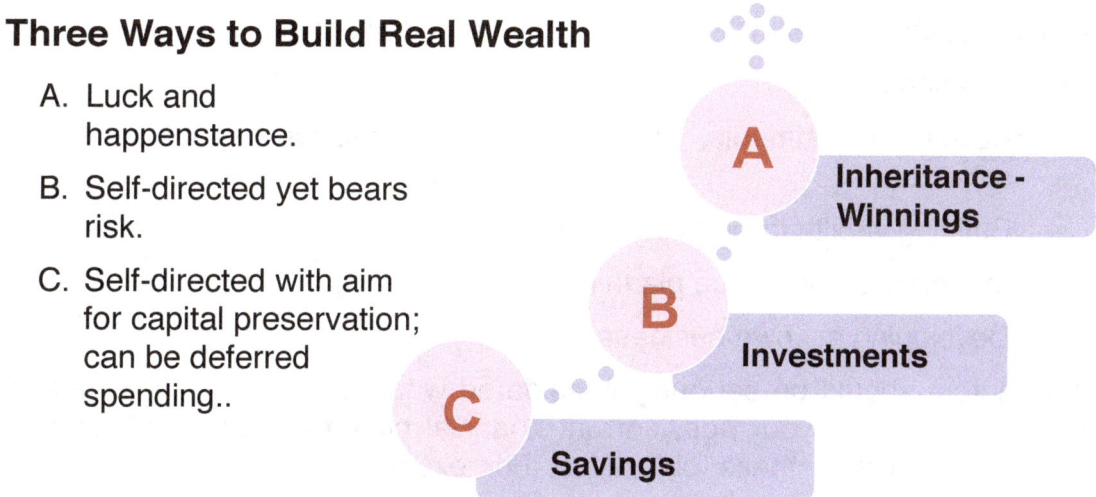

12.2 Faith-based Values in Wealth

Building Real Wealth as per Holy Scriptures

Primary sources offer instructions on allowable sources of income and earnings. For example, the Quran teaches:

> "And eat up not one another's property, unjustly, nor give bribery to the judges that you may knowingly eat up a part of the property of others sinfully." Al Baqarah V.2:188

> "Eat of the lawful things that We have provided you, with and be grateful to Allah." Al Baqarah V.2:172

After all, life-sustaining resources on earth are gifts from God:

> "He it is Who created for you all that is on earth." Al Baqarah V.2: 29

And hence are provided to all human beings as a matter of trust:

> "… and spend of that whereof He has made you trustees." Al Hadid V.57: 7

In this regard, we conclude that assets, wealth, and even knowledge must be safeguarded, protected, preserved, and ideally improved (e.g., shared), not wasted or squandered, nor exhausted in extravagance, nor hoarded for selfish ends.

Building Real Wealth

Creating wealth in a worldly, material sense can be accomplished by:

- Building savings
- Building investments, including through employer sponsors pension schemes
- Building wealth through insurance products
- Inheritance and estate planning
- Developing my own business

These factors should be seriously considered when laying down your financial objectives. Note that your age, current financial circumstances, and goals will influence and dictate these objectives. For example, younger people should emphasize capital growth and diversification, and as they approach retirement, shift to an emphasis on capital preservation and current income.

However, one should not ignore any of these important factors because they may negatively impact your accumulation of wealth and your ability to preserve capital. However, obviously not everyone is interested in or capable of launching their own business.

Because **Inheritance** and happenstance are uncertain and outside your control, let's now focus in and look more closely into how to build up real wealth through **Savings** and **Investments**, which are within your power and control.

12.3 Wealth-Building Through Savings

Saving money regularly is a patient and gradual, yet proven method to gain wealth. A rule of thumb is to target a savings goal of 5% to 10% of your gross annual income, divide this amount into monthly increments, then set it aside. Steady and regular savings can seem painful, especially at first, however, the payoff is the compounding effect of money making more money for you! (refer to next section for more on compounding)

While compound interest on debts (adding interest on top of interest) is prohibited for Muslims, the same principle can apply favorably for equity investments whereby dividends or income payouts can be re-invested into the same investment instrument and increase (compound) the invested value at a faster rate. The compound table below illustrates this point.

If you invest only the fixed amount stated in the table at the specified age and did not invest another dime, your wealth would grow by age 65 to the amount shown at bottom of the table, due to compounding and re-investment (assuming your invested funds grow at 10% annually).

Building Real Wealth - Savings

Amount Invested Today to Reach Savings Goal by Age 65
Amount Invested to be Compounded 10% per Year

Age	$228/Mo	$457/Mo	$914/Mo	$1,143/Mo
20	2,743	5,487	10,976	13,719
25	4,419	8,838	17,676	22,095
30	7,117	14,234	28,468	35,585
35	11,462	22,924	45,847	57,309
40	18,460	36,919	73,838	92,296
45	29,729	59,458	118,915	148,644
50	46,879	95,757	191,514	239,392
55	77,109	154,217	308,435	385,543
60	124,185	248,369	496,737	620,921
65	200,000	400,000	800,000	1,000,000

First Year Only

or Lump Sum there after

Question: Can you use this table below to calculate your future accumulated savings based on your current savings rate?

TIPS FOR SAVING SMART:

- Start as soon as possible
- Calculate your monthly cash flow and amount of "free" or disposable income that can be set aside as savings (refer to Chapter **7** – Budget)
- Establish savings targets
- <u>Pay yourself first</u> each month
- Contribute more to your savings account(s) whenever possible i.e., bonus, windfall funds, etc.
- Review your savings plan once per year for adjustments based on market conditions and prevailing risk factors

12.4 Wealth-Building Through Investments

Investments differ from savings in that investments typically involve the use of a financial instrument or vehicle (commonly a sophisticated one) which is managed by someone else and is exposed to some degree of risk. Savings are commonly managed by banks or credit unions where safety and liquidity are paramount, and risk exposure is minimal.

Investments include a broad range of securities such as shares, equities, bonds, modarabas, leases, real estate, commercial property, commodities-gold, etc.

It is important to gain an understanding of each type of investment vehicle, how it works, any inherent risk, the degree of liquidity, and the probable yield of the funds you invested.

Building Real Wealth - Savings

Types of Investments		Levels of Risk Associated with each type of Investment		
Money - Market / Deposits				
Land - Real Property				
Mudarabahs				
Leases / Ijara / Bonds /Sukuk				
Shares - Stocks				
	Low Risk	Medium Risk	High Risk	Highest Risk

This diagram above shows that level of risk (low to high) varies among the types of investment instruments.

Recall that there is a direct relationship between **Risk** and **Reward**:

High Risk = High Reward / Low Risk = Low Reward

First step always is to determine your risk appetite and risk tolerance before selecting the types of risk assets to invest in.

One needs additionally to have a general understanding of the concepts of financial markets (i.e., stocks, bonds, and mutual funds) to better appreciate the overall trend of investments and public expectations for profits. For example, in a "bear" or down market, it may be better to pursue a defensive strategy of capital preservation rather than accepting new or higher risks.

Always assess your attitude and tolerance for risk. This means, how much can you **afford to lose**? One cannot only focus on how much an investment will **gain in value.** Moreover, most types of investments require a degree of patience to realize their expected future value.

As such, there may be times when our investment valuation dips, but there is no need to panic if we had first evaluated the associated investment risk and are convinced of the inherent value in our underlying asset. Then, stay the course and be patient.

To summarize, the process of achieving wealth through **investments** is:

- Establish financial goals
- Evaluate your attitude to risk and the risk involved in the chosen form of investment
- Develop an investment strategy (conservative, balanced, growth, aggressive)
- Position your investments within your chosen strategy under a financial plan
- Implement your decisions and carefully monitor the results

12.5 Wealth-Building through Investments—Trade Off Risk and Return

The table below demonstrates the relationship between Risk and Return; specifically, that the higher the risk, the higher the rate of return. Conversely, the lower the risk, the lower the rate of return.

So, generally, low-risk investments are safer and produce a return that is more secure and more probable to occur as planned.

This next table shows the favorable results of investing $1.00 in various classes of securities in the United States, over the period 1926-1997. Again, shares or stocks offer much higher returns than their cash equivalent or bond counterparts.

Building Real Wealth – Investments
Trade Off Risk and Return

	1926-1977	1978-1997	1988-1997
Treasury Bills	14.25	4.08	1.70
Long-Term Govt Bond	39.07	7.22	2.97
S&P 500 (shares)	1,828.33	21.75	5.25
Small Cap Stocks	5,519.97	26.10	4.49
International Stocks	NA	14.70	1.89

For reference the average yield for Treasury bills in the period 2007 to 2013 which includes the Great Recession, or Global Financial Crisis, 4.9%; for S&P Shares is 9.8% ; and for Small Cap Stocks is 11%.

Trade Off Risk and Return

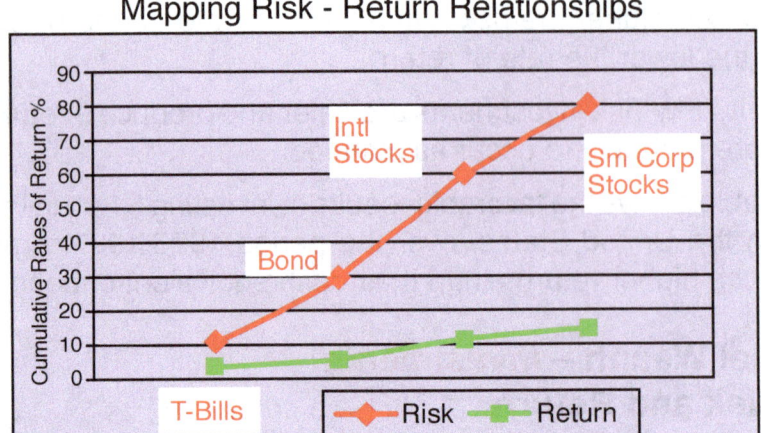

This diagram above shows graphically the less risky assets of treasury bills and money market funds that produce low returns of 10% over 5 years (with less risk), than international stocks with higher risk and average returns of 60% over 5+ years.

12.1 Exercise:

Describe the pros and cons of each type of investment instrument in the table. Consider the results and decide how you would allocate your investment funds in a way that is consistent with your personal risk tolerance.

In your comparison, examine these items: minimum and opening balances, services fees, withdrawal penalties or restrictions on access to your funds, yields and interest rates paid, various financial risks, etc.

Based on your research, place your investment decisions in the appropriate boxes to the right. What do you learn about personal risk tolerance?

Investments - Exercise

Exercise:

Instrument	What is it?	What is the risk?	What are the Pros?	What are the Cons?
Mutual Funds account				
Stocks and Shares				
Bonds				
Insurance Retirement Plan account				

Building Real Wealth – Investment Summary

Investing differs from **savings** by having long-term, more risk, and variable returns. Success with any Personal Wealth Plan is based on long-term investing.

An **investment** is anything that you purchase or acquire for future income or gain, whether recurring income (such as periodic rental income or dividends) or capital appreciation (such as an increase in stock value or land/real estate value at the time of resale).

Personal investing typically happens second, following an accumulation of money by **savings** which are set aside when you spend less than you earn. Deferred spending and gratification of desired results in "surplus" cash which can be segregated in a **savings** account for future use.

The first rule of building wealth is to preserve the principal amount, i.e., not to lose or devalue it. By practicing healthy money-saving habits (described in Chapter 5), you gradually add to the **savings** until these surplus funds become eligible for investing. Think of investing as a method to accelerate your rate of **savings**.

The placement of funds into investments involves risk. Either risk of principal and/or risk of expected returns/yields. Any appreciation in the market value of securities (capital gains) will increase your wealth portfolio and expand your net worth. However, it is worth noting that investments <u>do not always</u> go higher.

As we have seen, **savings** are generally for the short-term, involve little risk, and hence reap only modest returns—typically geared to the prevailing level of interest rates. Types of savings accounts include a bank saving deposit account, money market savings account, and certificate of deposit offered by banks.

Investing, on the other hand, involves a longer-term perspective, more risk, and generally uncertain returns. Smart investors realize that investing is <u>not</u> a get-rich-quick scheme. They choose to put money into investments regularly and keep it there for five, ten, fifteen, or more than twenty years to realize their financial goals.

> **General Disclaimer:** Information in this chapter on investing and elsewhere in this course/playbook was compiled from various sources and represents judgments, personal opinions, and experiences that might not produce the same outcomes for you. Of course, the author does not guarantee any particular results nor any profits from the implementation of the advice herein. While every effort was expended to be generally accurate and complete, the reader will be taking actions at their own discretion and is urged to seek out the advice of investing experts.

For building Real Wealth, then, there are simply two options:

1. Put your money to work through savings certificates on offer by banks usually with fixed returns (interest), or with variable profit-loss returns on offer by Islamic banks

   OR

2. Invest these funds with instruments yielding variable returns (and higher risk than savings) such as equities, shares, or mutual funds to generate more wealth sooner. Become familiar with concepts and tools of savings and rudimentary investing to bolster your confidence in basic money and asset management. Additional passive income earned from your savings ratios quickly tells the "story" of your personal financial health and will advance your march towards financial freedom!

12.2 Exercise:

Describe the pros and cons of each type of cash savings instrument.

Compare the results and decide how to allocate your savings funds in a way that is consistent with your personal risk tolerance.

Investments - Exercise

	Instrument	What is it?	What is the risk?	What are the Pros?	What are the Cons?
Exercise	Cash Saving account				
	Certificate of Deposit				
	Money Market account				
	Retirement account				

Note: Based upon your research: how would you choose to allocate your savings funds, considering both what you have learned and your personal risk tolerance?

Why Do Financial Statements Matter?

Provides a "snapshot" (or picture) of a moment in time of your financial situation. This picture can be taken privately, for yourself only, or to be shared with finance professionals like an asset manager or investment advisor.

Shows the general direction of your money habits and progression.

Gives an evaluation from the cash flow statement of how well you are managing the budget you established, and, most importantly, if the monthly cash flow is positive (surplus money) or negative (deficit money).

Ratios can be applied to the financial statements to compare with benchmarks—either your personal ones or industry standards—as explained in Chapter 9.

Practice preparing financial statements so when you need credit from banks you can easily supply them as an essential part of any application (and you will be well familiar with how the financial statements are prepared and how to read them).

12.6 Digital Money

BitCoin

A startling financial disruption occurred in 2009 with the advent of Bitcoin, the first crypto-currency and form of digital money. Bitcoin, like the imitators that have followed, utilizes the internet blockchain as a shared public ledger – meaning an open-source software program.

Hence, Bitcoin is a form of digital money circulating within a network of computers whereby transactions (buy-sell) are first confirmed and then recorded on a blockchain. These individual transactions are reflected in the buyer's or seller's electronic "wallet" on their personal digital device (such as phone, tablet or pc) that is typically also connected to a bank account.

Bitcoin

The real-time connection between the Bitcoin network and the individual wallet allows each coin to be validated and to update its value consistent with movements in the crypto-currency exchange up or down. See the graph below. Blockchain dynamics enforces a transparency, integrity and chronological order to all digital transactions – which is assured through cryptography, a method of data encryption which protects and secures the data. As of Q2 2021, the market value of all crypto-currencies is about $2 trillion dollars worldwide.

Below is a recent summary of market prices for Bitcoin since May 2020; reaching a market capitalization of $1 Tril for the first time.

Market cap of Bitcoin

The bitcoin price has soared by almost 700% since this time last year, with the bitcoin rally ... [+]   COINBASE

Since 2010, there are more than 1,800 crypto-currencies and private coins issued globally; of which some 500 have failed, gone bankrupt, been hacked or stolen, ended in scandal. Sadly, greed and other profiteering motives have destroyed many digital coins and private networks. Hence, both the high volatility of Bitcoin's market value and that of its imitators plus the numerous business failures underscores the risky nature of cryptos and has undermined public trust.

What is Digital Money?

Digital Money enables electronic payments in non-physical form—in contrast to fiat paper money. Instead of "hand-to-hand" payments by paper currency, checks or tangible metal coins, digital payments are affected by computers through mediums such as credit cards, smartphones, and online crypto-exchanges.

Cryptocurrency is nearly impossible to counterfeit or double-spend. Because its market value is set by a visible decentralized blockchain exchange, its purchasing power (value) is not subject to hoarding or manipulation. Generally, there are four levels of digital money:

- Coin issuers – Bitcoin, Ethereum, Ripple, Litecoin as examples
- Miners – people with huge computers systems solving mathematical puzzles that once solved releases new coins
- Payment gateways – PayPal being the most successful at offering a global payment service, or VISA, or MASTERCARD
- End Users – holders of digital or EWallets

So wherever online or in retail shops digital payments is accepted, the End Users can simply pay for goods and services using virtual money rather than carrying paper money and coins.

Initially, digital money is issued and circulates through private networks; however, during 2020-21 several national governments have concluded that a national crypto-currency is workable and these have issued a digital coin available on the blockchain and backed by trust in that nation's Central Bank. Examples here are: India, Singapore, PRC China, Japan, UAE, Venezuela, Estonia, Russia, Sweden.

Perceived Benefits and Risks

Among the perceived benefits of new digital money are:
- Convenience and ease of use (after a learning period)
- Security of payments
- Speedy and more affordable global or cross-border payments
- Integrity and transparency
- Less costly than bank and credit-card payments or wire transfers
- If using Bitcoin, anonymity when paying
- Once adopted, digital currencies can be issued by Central Banks are very low cost (CBDC – Central Bank Digital Currency)
- Governments can cheaply make social and relief payments to public to their phones or bank accounts

Whereas many observers point out these risks and perceived challenges with digital money:

- Dependency on private internet networks that are mostly unregulated
- Massive market volatility in coin values associated with rampant speculation
- Requires expensive electronic devices and access to wifi, internet
- Existing outside the normal banking system and vulnerable to being banned by national governments or Central Banks, thus becoming illegal to own
- Not immune to payment fraud and cyber-hacking
- Runs on data servers and hence open to breach and data theft or manipulation
- Early cryptos utilized by criminals and drug cartels for illegal payments

Future of Digital Money

Due to lower costs and higher security in issuance of currency when the format is digital money as opposed to fiat paper money, it is anticipated that many nations will embrace crypto-currency as the newest form of national legal tender for payments. Not everyone favors this outcome, however. Many people today are skeptical of losing direct ownership over the money in their pocket or wallet. Once paper cash is burned or destroyed, there is no going back. Realize that digital money may sit in your ewallet or digital bank account yet certainly you no longer control that data nor the purchasing power (value) of the digital money.

Because it is likely that digital money will be the only available form of money by 2030, it is highly recommended that you research cryptos and become more familiar with how your money is changing.

12.7 Chapter 12 Wrap Up – High Points Review

Intended Learning Outcomes:
- Become familiar with the three ways of building real wealth
- Understand the difference between savings and investments
- Describe the various types of savings options and basic rules to consider when building up personal savings
- Describe the various types of investment options and basic rules to consider when building up personal Investments
- Clarify what is meant by risk and return and distinguish between low-risk and high-risk types of investments
- Complete an exercise to make an asset allocation template for your investment portfolio based on your personal risk tolerances

MARVELOUS- YOU HAVE FINISHED CHAPTER 12 WITH AN IN-DEPTH DESCRIPTION OF WEALTH-BUILDING AND SUGGESTIONS FOR A STRATEGY TO BEGIN INVESTING. YOU NOW KNOW ABOUT RISK AND RETURN AND HAVE ASCERTAINED YOUR RISK TOLERANCE. STUNNING– 80% OF THIS PROGRAM IS DONE!

NOW MOVING ON....THE NEXT CHAPTER IS A GAP ANALYSIS (SIMILAR TO CHAPTER 4) WHERE YOU CAN COMPARE AND CONTRAST THE IMPORTANT GOALS SET IN CHAPTER 9 WITH YOUR PRESENT FINANCIAL RESULTS AND HAPPINESS LEVEL.

conscious wealth

visit

www.consciouswealth.me

Chapter 13

Gap Analysis

Quotes worth remembering...

"If past history was all that is needed to play the game of money, the richest people would be librarians."

— **Warren Buffett**

"Greatness begins beyond your comfort zone."

"Your excuses are just the lies your fears have sold you."

— **Robin Sharma**

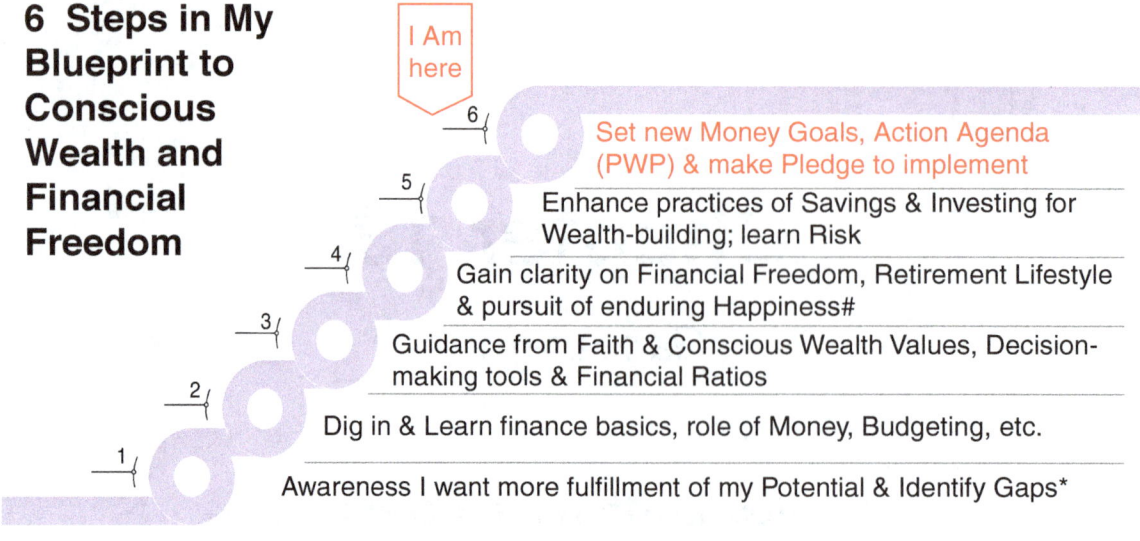

6 Steps in My Blueprint to Conscious Wealth and Financial Freedom

I Am here

6 — Set new Money Goals, Action Agenda (PWP) & make Pledge to implement

5 — Enhance practices of Savings & Investing for Wealth-building; learn Risk

4 — Gain clarity on Financial Freedom, Retirement Lifestyle & pursuit of enduring Happiness#

3 — Guidance from Faith & Conscious Wealth Values, Decision-making tools & Financial Ratios

2 — Dig in & Learn finance basics, role of Money, Budgeting, etc.

1 — Awareness I want more fulfillment of my Potential & Identify Gaps*

** Use Exercises to help find the Gaps.

#Includes Abundance Thinking which can be part of the last or first Step in this personal Journey yet essential quality to consistent, never-ending Self improvement.

13.0 What Are My Primary Outcomes of Chapter 13?

Analyze outcomes from Chapter **9 – Goal Setting** and Chapter **11 – Pursuit of Happiness**

Compare these sets of outcomes. What **gaps** do I notice?

Examine carefully:

> Where am I placing my central focus on daily basis?
>
> Where am I having success in realizing the results that I seek?
>
> What are the main obstacles keeping me from a forward trajectory?
>
> In which areas are my skills and talents inadequate and must be improved, updated, or expanded?
>
> What additional resources—money, possessions, people, and experiences—are necessary to help close the **gaps**?

13.1 Gap Analysis Basics

Describe the current situation of my reality.

Describe in some detail the desired reality...what is the ideal future I am moving towards?

When comparing these two pictures, what stands out as not aligned? What is aligned and yet not the anticipated quantity (i.e., not yet enough)?

Where are the gaps—the largest differences? The smallest differences?

13.2 A Template to Consider Gaps

Stretch my imagination to identify the nature of the **gap**, and reflect on what can be done to narrow or fully close each **gap**.

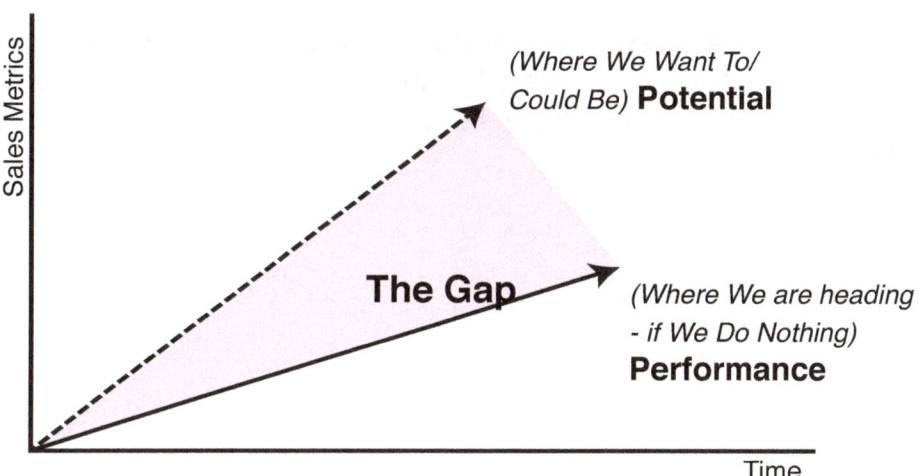

A template from sales to help consider Gaps

Next, set priorities. Perhaps certain **gaps** will only be closed once other aspects have evolved. For example, running hurdles faster requires X number of hours of practice on the course for familiarization and augmenting courage.

If reducing certain **gaps** necessitates time and money, then allocate a budget to make that investment.

Recall that intentions must be anchored in <u>commitment</u> (perseverance) and <u>actions</u> to become a new reality. Wishful thinking is not enough.

This exercise is similar to that in Chapter 4.

Exercise 13.1 **List the main new beliefs I must have to advance.**

Next, identify the new Beliefs that I must hold about myself, about my environment, about my current reality, to make me receptive to changes and to make a way open for the arrival of the new reality. This is the reaction in the **Law of Attraction** (a Universal Law) to my thinking my personal desires onto the formless Substance.

....

....

....

....

....

....

Modifying existing beliefs (established starting in infancy and early childhood) often takes time and practice to reset the brain patterns in support of the new desired reality. Stay committed, and believe these changes can occur to reduce the gaps identified.

13.3 Thinking into Results

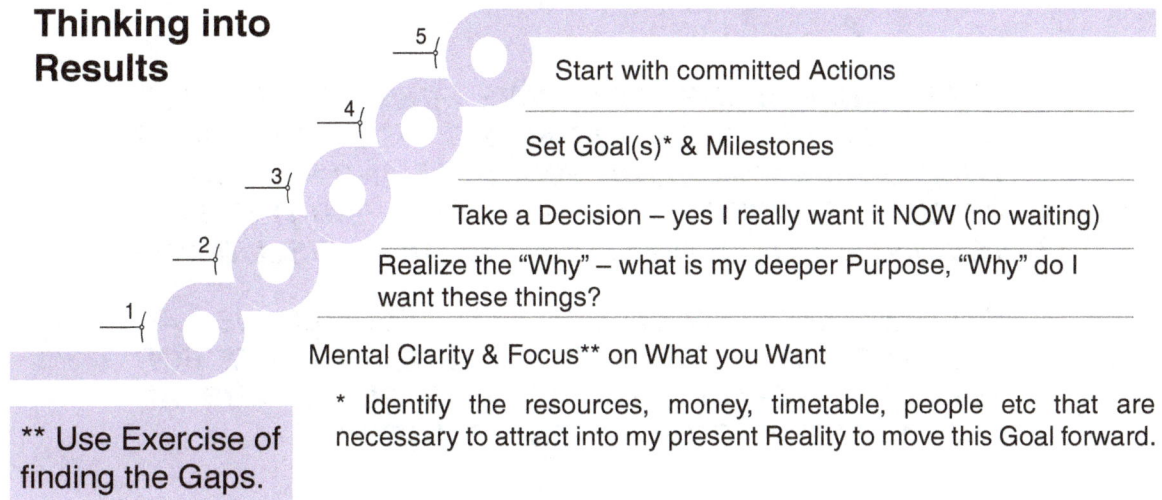

Thinking into Results

5 — Start with committed Actions
4 — Set Goal(s)* & Milestones
3 — Take a Decision – yes I really want it NOW (no waiting)
2 — Realize the "Why" – what is my deeper Purpose, "Why" do I want these things?
1 — Mental Clarity & Focus** on What you Want

* Identify the resources, money, timetable, people etc that are necessary to attract into my present Reality to move this Goal forward.

** Use Exercise of finding the Gaps.

Having identified and listed my beliefs about myself and my circumstances that must change in order to "close the gap" between my performance/results and my goals, then I now need to focus upon thinking this into results.

The simple diagram above demonstrates the mental steps and progression to commence this process of manifesting what I really want- 'thinking into results".

Like everything else, this cannot occur without changing my paradigm AND taking persistent actions.

13.4 Chapter 13 Wrap Up – High Points Review

Intended Learning Outcomes:

Completed an analysis of the outcomes from Chapter **9 – Goal Setting** and Chapter **11 – Pursuit of Happiness and examined any gaps that are found.**

Made careful examination of my central focus, in which areas I am experiencing success, alternatively in which areas there seem to be obstacles or roadblocks, and reflect on what must change to get "unstuck" and build momentum going forward.

FORMIDABLE WORK- YOU HAVE FINISHED CHAPTER 13 BY MAKING A GAP ANALYSIS THAT COMPARES YOUR GOALS WITH YOUR FINANCIAL AND HAPPINESS RESULTS. CONSEQUENTLY, YOU WILL FIND IT EASIER TO ADJUST GOALS OR CLOSE THE GAPS. WELL DONE!

NOW MOVING ON...THE NEXT CHAPTER IS AN ACTION CHAPTER THAT PROVIDES A TEMPLATE FOR YOU TO DEVELOP BOTH ACTIONS PLANS AND AN ACCOMPANYING GOAL-ORIENTED AGENDA.

conscious wealth

visit

www.consciouswealth.me

Chapter 14

Action Agenda and Plan

Quotes worth remembering…

"I always knew I was going to be rich. I don't think I ever doubted it for a minute."
— **Warren Buffett**

"Having talent is fantastic. Having confidence is even more important."

"The way we do small things determines the way we do everything."
— **Robin Sharma**

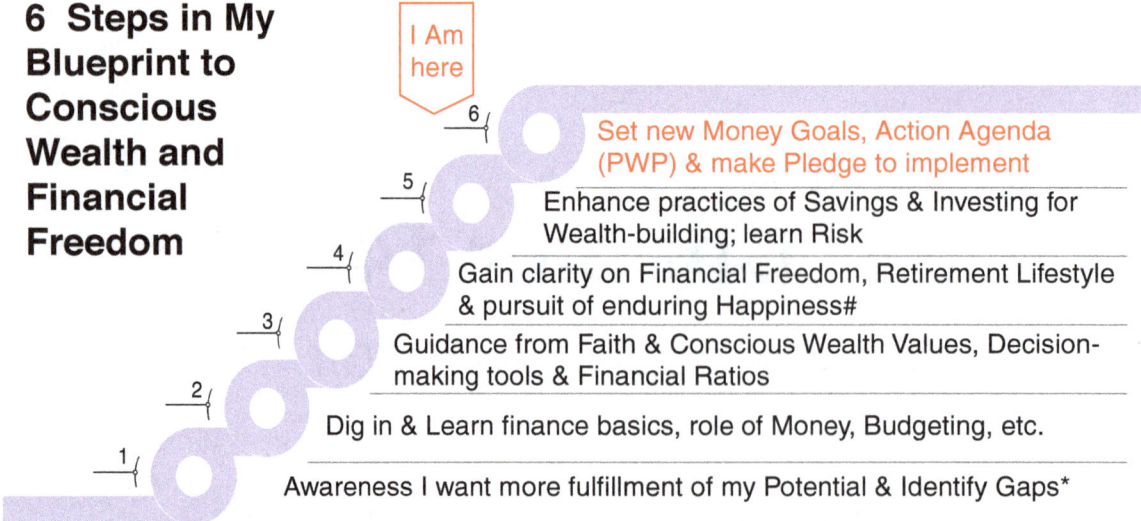

** Use Exercises to help find the Gaps.

#Includes Abundance Thinking which can be part of the last or first Step in this personal Journey yet essential quality to consistent, never-ending Self improvement.

14.0 What Are My Primary Outcomes of Chapter 14?

- Define personal action agenda and its components
- Clearly understand the six segments of an action agenda and where to look for the financial information to fill each to completion
- Review the main troubleshooting steps and what to look out for
- Identify four potential obstacles to avoid when implementing an action agenda
- Review using hints about financial planning which could be incorporated into my personal action agenda

14.1 What is an Action Agenda?

This Chapter ties together the results of the past thirteen lessons into a coherent plan which we shall call a "Personal Action Agenda".

Refer to the excel spreadsheet in the Appendix labeled "Personal Action Agenda" throughout this section. The Personal Action Agenda (PAA) consists of six segments. Describing them from left to right:

Action Steps to be Taken – this is a short narrative of the concrete steps to be taken by you (and your spouse/family), broken down into a short-term time horizon (1-6 months and 7-12 months), medium-term time horizon (2-3 years) and long-term time horizon (4 years and beyond).

What Financial Subject or Items are Impacted – credit cards, savings account, education fund, hajj fund, etc.

Goals/Objectives – described in figures: $3,000 pay-off of loan(s); $2,000 increase to education fund, etc.

Short-Term Objectives in figures for 1-6 months and 7-12 months

Medium-Term Objectives in figures for 2-3 years

Long-Term Objectives for 4 years and beyond

It is very important to write down your objectives and place them on a realistic timeline, so this can form a To Do list and serve to remind you on the milestones intended to be realized and by when.

How to Complete the Personal Action Agenda:

Exercise 14.1

First, place the disposable cash flow result (appendix: see cash flow worksheet) in Cell E10. This is your starting point for the Personal Action Agenda.

Identify the various actions and decisions that you want to be part of your Personal Action Agenda to move closer to your desired results. Be as specific as possible, quantify the goals into figures and put a deadline with dates wherever possible.

Next, calculate the savings and investment financial goals (or objectives) that you desire, noting how much you want to save each month by a specific date. From there, assign your specific financial goals to a timeframe and work backward to the present day to determine how much you need to save/pay each month starting from now to achieve your desired goal. Refer to the factor of compound profits Chapter 7.

Finally, review the resultant Personal Action Agenda at least once per month to see your progress, or to spot variances from your plan and then adjust accordingly to get back on track.

Troubleshooting the Action Agenda

Troubleshooting your Personal Action Agenda starts with a realization that oftentimes even the best of intentions may not allow you to "stay the course" and you may discover that you have deviated from your plan, or worse yet, abandoned the plan altogether.

The following list of helpful hints should assist you in staying on course and give you the patience to allow the plan to work until your desired goals are realized.

- **Pay YOURSELF first** each month
- Pay off the largest bills and personal debts before you add to a new Savings account or fund
- Forego some discretionary spending, reduce the consumption spending each month to have more money to set aside into savings/investing

Be patient with your Action Agenda and plana. Give them time to accumulate money and increase in value (see Chapter 9).

Sometimes the best of intentions and actions seem to be blocked by circumstances. Gear up your patience and resolve to press onwards when the situation changes to be more favorable. There's no sense in rowing upstream against the current.

If you have abandoned the monthly savings plan, examine why this is: was the monthly target too high? Unrealistic? If so, then reduce the monthly savings target amount and immediately re-start the plan.

14.2 Potential Action Agenda Obstacles to Avoid

A lack of clarity can be avoided by a review of Chapter 9 for setting SMART goals and milestones.

"Chunk down" the work ahead—don't try to take on too much at once

Identify the signs of feeling overwhelmed: confusion, vacillation, negative thoughts, surging feelings of frustration, or even short bursts of anger. At these moments, pause, breathe deeply, re-set your attitude, and re-focus on your primary **goals**, rather than the **obstacles** that may have appeared.

Ignore the advice from loved ones where the message is: "you can't really do this; your goal is impossible". Similar opinions might be intended to help you but they will only stir up doubts and lack of focus.

<u>Summary</u>: Components of a Personal Financial Plan may look like the next graphic.

Framework of a Personal Financial Plan

- Understand "Matrix of Starting Points"
- Set Financial Objectives
- Manage (any) loans and debts
- Grow money knowledge
- Learn savings habits and invest

Framework of a Personal Financial Plan - 2

- Learn risk tolerance and build confidence to invest by accepting risk

- Identify and leverage opportunities as these arise

- Protect your wealth as assets grow

Hints and reminders of the key elements of your Action Agenda:

Restated here are the **8 key components for financial planning you will need to consider:**

- Budgeting to include:
    1. repeat and recurring expenses
    2. one-time and annual expenses, like taxes
- Managing liquidity, or ready access to cash
- Financing large purchases
- Managing your risk
- Investing your money
- **Set goals to a retirement** plan (expected date and pension nest-egg amount)
- Outline goal(s) for the eventual transfer of your wealth to heirs
- Organized record keeping

What are the **ten basic principles of sound personal financial management?**

1. Organize your finances. Organizing your finances is the first step to creating wealth
2. Develop a budget, income statement, balance sheet and inventory of assets and liabilities
3. Spend less than I earn
4. Be SMART: put my money to work for me, start saving
5. Limit **debt** to income-producing **assets**
6. Continuously educate yourself
7. Learn and seek to understand risk and my appetite for risk
8. Develop an Action Agenda.
9. Diversification and spread of risk for my investments
10. Always maximize my employment benefits because I deserve them

14.3 Once Again, Concluding Words to the Wise

"The principles always work if you work the principles!" Jack Canfield

Don't blame the past; the past is perfect as it has brought you to this moment—poised for personal transformation. Be ready to learn more!

Celebrate a new awareness; change in personal habits is never easy. Our "old, comfortable self" constantly pulls us back into that familiar comfort zone. Yet, it is always possible to break through this familiarity and find new ways of doing things.

Try on the new wings—become free and liberated from past limitations and advance towards your true self.

Remember that success takes time and perseverance. This is not necessarily hard work, but steady, forward momentum into new habits and ideals, coping with inevitable challenges, changes, and obstacles, as well as dealing with disappointment and mistakes that arise. The key is determination and practice, practice, practice.

Develop a network of support: like any journey, going at it alone is tough, so choose friends, family, relatives, and colleagues who empathize with your desire for personal change and can form a support system to assist, offer advice, encouragement, and help mobilize resources, information and solutions to resolve frustrations and quickly overcome temporary "failures".

Note: this process is not automatic. Individual results are determined by individual actions—you must do the work. However, individuals can save up to ten years by learning from and using proven models of financial learning set out by masters.

14.4 Chapter 14 Wrap Up – High Points review

Intended Learning Outcomes:

- Define personal action agenda and its components
- Clearly understand the six segments of an action agenda and where to look for the financial information to fill each to completion
- Review the main troubleshooting steps and what to look out for
- Identify four potential obstacles to avoid when implementing an action agenda Review using hints about financial planning which could be incorporated into my personal action agenda

MAGNIFICENTLY DONE! YOU HAVE FINISHED CHAPTER 14 AND NOW UNDERSTAND HOW TO PREPARE BOTH AN ACTION AGENDA – REPLETE WITH IMPORTANT FINANCIAL AND OTHER PERSONAL GOALS-- AND A TEMPLATE OF ACTION PLANS WITH TIMELINES. THESE TOOLS CAN HELP LAUNCH YOU ON A PATHWAY TO WEALTH AND PERSONAL SUCCESS. WELL DONE!

NOW MOVING ON...THE NEXT CHAPTER IS THE FINAL CHAPTER OF THE ROADMAP TO SEAL YOUR RESOLVE TO APPLY YOUR NEWLY ACQUIRED FINANCIAL KNOWLEDGE AND SKILLS TO CO-CREATE A BRIGHTER FUTURE! YOU'VE GOT THIS!

conscious wealth

visit

www.consciouswealth.me

Chapter 15

My Pledge

Quotes worth remembering…

"You only have to do a very few things right in your life so long as you don't do too many things wrong."

"The most important investment you can make is in yourself."

— **Warren Buffett**

"Make your faith larger than your fears and your dreams bigger than your doubts."

"It's not about the end goal, it's about who you become by consistently pushing to the edge of your limits."

— **Robin Sharma**

6 Steps in My Blueprint to Conscious Wealth and Financial Freedom

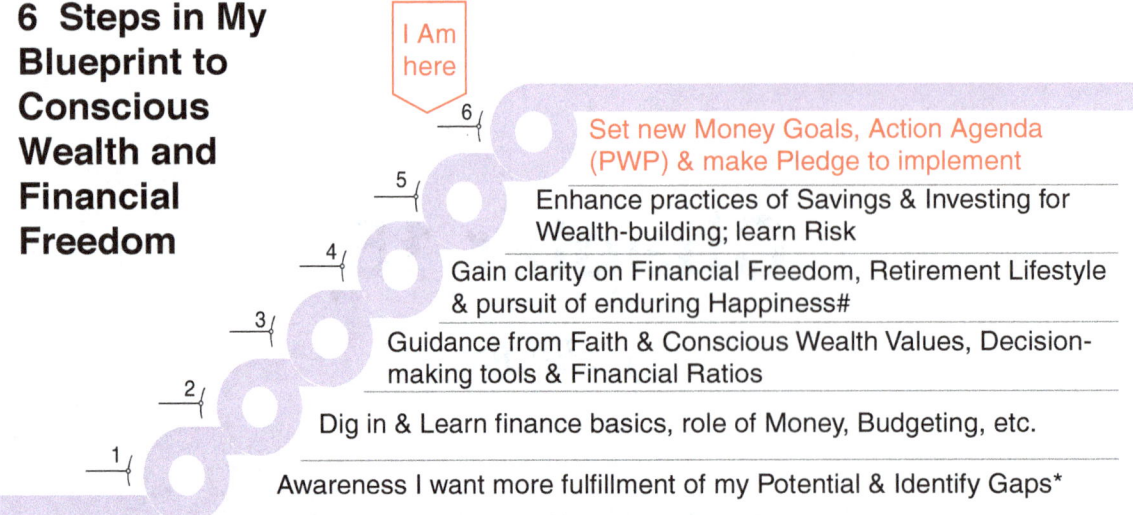

6. Set new Money Goals, Action Agenda (PWP) & make Pledge to implement
5. Enhance practices of Savings & Investing for Wealth-building; learn Risk
4. Gain clarity on Financial Freedom, Retirement Lifestyle & pursuit of enduring Happiness#
3. Guidance from Faith & Conscious Wealth Values, Decision-making tools & Financial Ratios
2. Dig in & Learn finance basics, role of Money, Budgeting, etc.
1. Awareness I want more fulfillment of my Potential & Identify Gaps*

** Use Exercises to help find the Gaps.

#Includes Abundance Thinking which can be part of the last or first Step in this personal Journey yet essential quality to consistent, never-ending Self improvement.

15.0 What Are My Primary Outcomes of Chapter 15?

- Make a primary commitment to myself, called "My Pledge". Now that the learning in this caching program is completed, the time has arrived for implementation.
- Add my name to the pledge card. Add a date for starting.
- Once filled in, attach my pledge to a copy of my PWP.
- Also, a copy of this pledge can be reduced to the size of an index card to fit into my pocket or purse for easy reading several times each day.

15.1 How to Do My Pledge of Commitment

Identify what short-term goal(s) I am now intending to action and realize. Once implementation commences, I can focus on a range of activities and decisions to build up momentum towards realization, which will assist with feelings of satisfaction and achievement.

As a wise man said: "Beginning the job is more than half done."

If I can muster up great self-discipline, then **my pledge** may be enough to encourage me off the starting blocks and burst out the gate. Or consider asking a close friend (or coach) to be an **accountability buddy** to periodically check on my implementation progress. External accountability partners have proven to be highly productive when making behavior changes.

Now it's time to fill in **my pledge** and get going!

Exercise 15.1

Now that I am a graduate of the Coaching Wheel Program, I hereby Pledge my Commitment…

Exercise

> **My Pledge**
>
> I, _____ (name), Pledge that I am now committed to implement the first Phase of my Personal Wealth Plan (PWP) starting on this date _____.
>
> **Conscious Wealth Coaching Program**
>
> iwealth

Congratulations! Now I am a graduate of the Coaching Wheel Program.

I feel fully empowered to implement the Roadmap that I developed starting today!

15.2 Chapter 15 Wrap Up – High Points review

Intended Learning Outcomes:

- Make a primary commitment to myself called, "**My Pledge**". Now that I am a graduate of the Coaching Wheel Program and the entire 15 Chapters are complete, the time has arrived to shift from learning to implementation.
- Add my name to the pledge card. Add a date for starting implementation.
- Once filled in, attach M**y Pledge** to a copy of my PWP, action agenda, action plans, and personal financial statements.

SO IMPRESSIVE- YOU HAVE JUST FINISHED CHAPTER 15 AND THE FULL 6 STEPS OF THIS PROGRAM. THIS IS THE RIGHT TIME TO AFFIRM A SOLEMN PLEDGE TO YOURSELF THAT THERE ARE NO MORE EXCUSES, NO GOING BACKWARDS, NO MORE DAY-DREAMING... INSTEAD, YOU ARE FIRMLY COMMITTED TO ADVANCING FORWARD TOWARDS THE BEST VERSION OF YOU!

ARMED WITH RENEWED CONFIDENCE AND NEW SKILLS IN MONEY MATTER, YOU SEE A CLEAR PATHWAY FORWARD TO FULFILL YOUR FULL POTENTIAL, ACCELERATE WEALTH-BUILDING AND DISCOVER ENDURING HAPPINESS. WELL DONE!

visit

www.consciouswealth.me

Final Exercise 15.2 List the main new Beliefs I must have to advance

This is what I now believe to be true:

For example– "I attract money needed to lessen debts and boost savings…"

1. ……………………………………………
2. ……………………………………………
3. ……………………………………………
4. ……………………………………………
5. ……………………………………………
6. ……………………………………………
7. ……………………………………………

iwealth

Feel free to add affirmations or additional paper to write out all the new beliefs. Review these often.

CONCLUSION

Congratulations on completing the 15-Chapter personal journey to financial intelligence! By now, you are prepared to meet any challenge head-on for a brighter financial future with:

- A personal inventory of unique talents, gifts. and assets/liabilities
- clarity of your true desires
- a deeper understanding of your relationship to money and its role in your life
- personalized financial statements: balance sheet, income statement, cash flow, monthly budget
- faith-based guidance to thrive with money
- insights into goal setting and financial ratios
- knowledge to calculate your point of **financial freedom** and retirement savings
- guidance on how to transform a mental paradigm
- traits for exceptional living and <u>sustained</u> **happiness**

The mission of this non-technical, highly interactive **Conscious Wealth** coaching program is not simply to reinvent financial literacy but also to teach life-changing tools and techniques for overcoming money struggles and substituting healthy money habits.

Throughout the 15 Chapters, dear reader, you encountered fun, colorful, appealing, and informative templates and exercises designed to allow you to generate a new money roadmap that steers you towards increased wealth, less stress, and more success.

We care about your journey forward. Please contact us in 3-6 months (or sooner) with your money story. Tell us what changed, what improved, what wealth gains have been realized etc. Don't blame the past or remain stuck... instead, seize this coaching program as an opportunity to reshape your relationship with money. All worthwhile personal achievements take time and effort, so why not begin the work today?

If you want in-person coaching or one-to-one virtual coaching please reach out to: **www.consciouswealth.me** or email us at **omar@consciouswealth.me**. Our entire financial intelligence team is ready to assist you.

Appendix

ITEM #1. Action Agenda Sample (A)

				SHORT TERM	
Disposable income (from Cash Flow Sheet)		SR 2603 E10 = $ 694.13		1 to 6 mos Financial Targets	7 to 12 Mos Financial Targets
Column A	Column B	Column C	Column D	Column E	Column F
ACTION STEPS TO BE TAKEN	SUBJECT / FINANCIAL ITEMS	GOALS / OBJECTIVES			
		Mo. Savings	Mo. Payoff		
1. SHORT - TERM					
2. Pay Off	Credit Cards = 40,000		3,000		2,000
3. Pay Off	Personal Loans / Debts				-
4. Start Savings - Investment Plan					-
5. Set Aside Cash for 3 Mos.	Emergency Fund = 15,000	2,400			2,400
6. Acquire Additional Life Insurance	Term Protection = 100,000				
7. Acquire Indiv. Disability Insurance		400			-
8. Start College / University Savings Plan	Target Ed. Fund = 25,000	3,000		3,000	3,000
9. Convert Term Life insurance to Cash Value Policy					
11. MEDIUM - TERM					
12. Save Funds for Hajj, or Umrah travel to Mekkah	Target Hajj Fund = 8,000	700		2,000	6,000
13. Save Funds to Purchase First Home					
14. Save Funds for Marriage					
15. Save Funds for Education/Fund No. 2					
16. Accumulate Funds to Acquire a Business					
17. Start a Saving Plan for Vacation Home	Target House Fund = 20,000				
18. Accumulate Funds to buy Commercial Property					
19. LONGER - TERM					
20. Contribute to individual Retirement Plan	Target Retirement Plan = 1,200,000	2,000			
21. Save to Acquire a Retirement Home					
22. Retire at 65	Target = 60,0000 Annual Income				
23. Maintain Pre-Retirement Standard of Living during Retirement Years				25,000	50,000
24. Maintain Quality of Healthcare during Retirement					
25. Totals:					

STEPS:
1. Place Disposable Cash Flow Result (see Cash Flow Worksheet) in Cell E10. This is Your Starting Point.
2. Identify the various Actions that You Want to be part of Your Personal Action Agenda... be as specific as possible, quantify and put deadline dates.
3. Calculate the Financial Goals or Objectives that You Desire... say how much to Save Monthly and by When.
4. Assign Your Specific Financial Goal to a Time Frame and work backwards to the Present Day to determine how much You need to Pay / Save each month starting from now.
5. Review Your Personal Action Agenda at least Monthly to see Your Progress or to spot variances from Your Plan and make adjustments accordingly.

CONSCIOUS WEALTH

	SHORT TERM		SHORT TERM		MEDIUM TERM			LONG TERM			
	1 to 6 Mos Monthly Budget	One-Time Budget	7 to 12 Mos Monthly Budget	One-Time Budget	2Yr Financial Targets	3Yr Financial Targets	4Yr Financial Targets	5Yr Financial Targets	7Yr Financial Targets	10Yr Financial Targets	15Yr Financial Targets
	Column G	Column H	Column I	Column J	Column K	Column L	Column M	Column N	Column O	Column P	Column Q
		3,000		333			500				
	-										
	2,400	400		400							
		2,000									
	-										
	500		500								
		2,000	1,000								
						3,500					
	2,000							25,000 up to 12 yrs			
	4,167	25,000	4,167	25,000	90,000	150,000	210,000	275,000	425,000	600,000	minimum
	7,400	29,000	6,567	25,000							

ITEM #2. Action Agenda Blank worksheet (B)

				SHORT TERM	
				1 to 6 mos Financial Targets	7 to 12 Mos Financial Targets
Disposable income (from Cash Flow Sheet)		SR 2603 E10 = $ 694.13			
Column A ACTION STEPS TO BE TAKEN	Column B SUBJECT / FINANCIAL ITEMS	Column C GOALS / OBJECTIVES	Column D	Column E	Column F
		Mo. Savings	Mo. Payoff		
1. SHORT - TERM					
2. Pay Off					
3. Pay Off					
4. Start Savings - Investment Plan					
5. Set Aside Cash for 3 Mos.					
6.					
7.					
8.					
9.					
11. MEDIUM - TERM					
12. Save Funds for Hajj, or Umrah travel to Mekkah					
13.					
14.					
15.					
16.					
17.					
18.					
19. LONGER - TERM					
20. Contribute to individual Retirement Plan					
21.					
22.					
23.					
24					
25. Totals:					

STEPS:

1. Place Disposable Cash Flow Result (see Cash Flow Worksheet) in Cell E10. This is Your Starting Point.
2. Identify the various Actions that You Want to be part of Your Personal Action Agenda... be as specific as possible, quantify and put deadline dates.
3. Calculate the Financial Goals or Objectives that You Desire... say how much to Save Monthly and by When.
4. Assign Your Specific Financial Goal to a Time Frame and work backwards to the Present Day to determine how much You need to Pay / Save each month starting from now.
5. Review Your Personal Action Agenda at least Monthly to see Your Progress or to spot variances from Your Plan and make adjustments accordingly.

SHORT TERM		SHORT TERM		MEDIUM TERM				LONG TERM		
1 to 6 Mos Monthly Budget	One-Time Budget	7 to 12 Mos Monthly Budget	One-Time Budget	2Yr Financial Targets	3Yr Financial Targets	4Yr Financial Targets	5Yr Financial Targets	7Yr Financial Targets	10Yr Financial Targets	15Yr Financial Targets
Column G	Column H	Column I	Column J	Column K	Column L	Column M	Column N	Column O	Column P	Column Q

ITEM #3. Risk Budget blank worksheet

REAL ASSETS AND PROPERTY
Hint: To find Value refer to Balance Sheet or Cash Flow Worksheet

#	Ref	Item	Basis
1.	BS24	Prime Residence/Home	Replacement Cost
2.	BS25	Second Residence/Vacation Home	Replacement Cost
3.	BS17	Personal Property /Rental	Replacement Cost
4.	BS17	Commercial Property	Replacement Cost
5.	BS26	Home Furnishings	Replacement Cost
6.	BS30	Boat/Plane	Market Value
7.	BS27	Jewelry	Market Value
8.	BS28	Collectibles/Art/Antique	Market Value
9.	BS29	Autos	Market VAlue/Depreciation
10.	BS30	Other real Assets	

FINANCIAL ASSETS AND INVESTMENTS

#	Ref	Item	Basis
11.	BS1-8	Savings Account	Market Value
12.	BS1 or 3	Emergency Funds	Net Asset Value
13.	BS9	Cash Value Insurance	Net Asset Value
14.	BS11	Stocks/Shares (current Market Value)	Market Value
15.	BS12	Bonds	Market Value
16.	BS13	Mutual Funds	Net Asset Value
17.	BS14	Hajj/Umrah Funds	Net Asset Value
18.	BS15	Partnership Interest	Cost Basis
19.	BS16	Business Enterprise Ownership	Market Value
20.	BS18 or 20	Retirement Funds/Pensions	Net Asset Value
21.	BS21	Employee Savings Accounts	Net Asset Value
22.	BS22	Other Long Term Retirement Plans	Net Asset Value
23.	BS30	Book Royalties/Patents/Inventions	Market Value
24.	BS19	Other Investments	

HEALTH-MEDICAL AND WELL-BEING

#	Ref	Item	Basis
25.	CF31	Prescription Drugs/Vitamins	Estimated Medical Costs
26.	CF31	preventive Medical Care	Estimated Medical Costs
27.		Accidents/Illness/Sickness	Estimated Medical Costs
28.	CF24	Disability – Partial or Total (unable to work)	Annual Income Multiple
29.	CF24	Long Term Care/Old Age	Estimated Medical Costs
30.		Death	Funeral/Burial Expenses
31.		Inheritance Gifts	
32.	CF34	Zakat Obligation	Shariah Calculation
33.	CF35	Hajj Pilgrimage	Market Value
34.	CF33	Sadaqa	
35.	CF33	Sadaqa Jarayia	

Totals

Insurable Valuation Guide Covered Value	Existing or Estimated Interest/ Insurance Premium	Type of Risk Protection
		General Takaful/Personal Lines
		General Takaful/Personal Lines
		General Takaful/Personal Lines
		General Takaful/Commercial Lines
		General Takaful/Personal Lines
		General Takaful/Personal Lines
		Gen Takaful/PersLine/Fine Arts
		Gen Takaful/Personal Lines
		Auto/Liability
		None
		None
		None
		None
		None
		None
		None
		Bull-Sell Agreement – BusinessMan Coverage
		Bull-Sell Agreement – BusinessMan Coverage
		None
		None
		None
		None
		Health Care Coverage
		Takaful/Critical Illness
		Takaful/Disability
		Health Care Coverage
		Takaful/Life Cover
		Savings Plan
		None
		Savings Plan
		None

Disclaimer: This Worksheet is for information purposes only and does not purport to give investment, tax or any other specialized advice. The author does not accept any responsibility or liability for errors or inaccuracies made by users.

ITEM #4. Sources and Uses Monthly Sample worksheet

SOURCES – INCOME			% of Income
1. PERIODIC OR FIXED		INPUT VALUES	
2. Salary/Earnings:	Earner 1	7,000	
	Earner 2	0	
3. Rents and Royalties		0	
4. Pension Income		0	
5. Trust Income		0	
6. Stipends		0	
7. Subtotal		7,000	(7/20) = 5.6%
8. SEASONAL OR VARIABLE			
9. Self-employment Income		0	
10. Production/Bonuses		15,000	
11. Vacation/Ramada Bonuses		25,000	
12. Commissions			
13. Subtotal		40,000	(13/20) = 32.2%
14. SAVINGS/INVESTMENT INCOME			
15. Dividends		0	
16. Capital Gains		0	
17. Interest Earnings*		0	
18. Other Income		0	
19 Subtotal		0	(19/21) = 0.0%
20. Total Regular Cash Available		2,500	124,000
USES – EXPENSES			
21. PERIODIC OR FIXED	(Remember Inputs from MoExpo Sheet!)		
22. Housing/Prime/Secondary		1,850	
23. Insurance Premium/Property		200	
24. Insurance Premium/Personal		1,090	
25. Subtotal		3,140	(25/38) = 27.1%
26. SEASONAL OR VARIABLE			
27. Food/Groceries		2,000	
28. Transportation – Commuting		2,000	
29. Debt – Obligations Payment		1,000	
30. Provision for Income Tax (if any)		—	
31. Medical Expenses			
32. Education (Current Expenses)		1,300	
33. Charitable Donations – Good Deeds		360	
34. Zakat Obligations			
35. Other Personal Items		0	
36. Other Monthly Expenses/Savings (less insur prem)		1,800	
37. Subtotal		8,460	(37/38) = 72.9%
38. Total Monthly Expenses		11,600	
39. Annual	(38 X 12) = 139,200		
40. Net Cash Flow (Monthly Surplus: {inflow+/outflow-})	(7-38) = -4,600		
41. Annual	(20-39) = -15,200		

*Disclaimer: This Worksheet is for information purposes only and does not purport to give investment, tax or any other specialized advice. The author does not accept any responsibility or liability for errors or inaccuracies made by users.

ITEM #5. Sources and Uses Monthly blank worksheet

SOURCES – INCOME				% of Income
1. PERIODIC OR FIXED		INPUT VALUES		
2. Salary/Earnings:	Earner 1			
	Earner 2			
3. Rents and Royalties				
4. Pension Income				
5. Trust Income				
6. Stipends				
7. Subtotal				
8. SEASONAL OR VARIABLE				
9. Self-employment Income				
10. Production/Bonuses				
11. Vacation/Ramada Bonuses				
12. Commissions				
13. Subtotal				
14. SAVINGS/INVESTMENT INCOME				
15. Dividends				
16. Capital Gains				
17. Interest Earnings*				
18. Other Income				
19. Subtotal				
20. Total Regular Cash Available				
USES – EXPENSES				
21. PERIODIC OR FIXED		*(Remember Inputs from MoExpo Sheet!)*		
22. Housing/Prime/Secondary				
23. Insurance Premium/Property				
24. Insurance Premium/Personal				
25. Subtotal				
26. SEASONAL OR VARIABLE				
27. Food/Groceries				
28. Transportation – Commuting				
29. Debt – Obligations Payment				
30. Provision for Income Tax (if any)				
31. Medical Expenses				
32. Education (Current Expenses)				
33. Charitable Donations – Good Deeds				
34. Zakat Obligations				
35. Other Personal Items				
36. Other Monthly Expenses/Savings (less insur prem)				
37. Subtotal				
38. Total Monthly Expenses				
39. Annual				
40. Net Cash Flow (Monthly Surplus: {inflow+/outflow-})				
41. Annual				

* *Disclaimer: This Worksheet is for information purposes only and does not purport to give investment, tax or any other specialized advice. The author does not accept any responsibility or liability for errors or inaccuracies made by users.*

ITEM #6. Balance Sheet sample (A1)

BALANCE SHEET

ASSETS The things that I own	2006 SR	% of Assets
1. Savings: Cash	40,000	
2. Checking Accounts	5,000	
3. Money Market Accounts	-	
4. Money Market Funds	6,000	
5. Certificates of Deposit	-	
6. Gold / Commodities (Mkt value)	-	
7. Mudarabahs		
8. Treasury Notes/Bills		
9. Cash Value of Life Insurance	-	
10. Total Current Assets	51,000	(10/32) = 7.1%
11. Investments: Stocks/Shares	37,500	
12. Bonds/Soukuks	-	
13. Mutual Funds (current mkt value)	-	
14. Hajj / Umrah Savings Account	-	
15. Partnership Interests	-	
16. Business Enterprise Ownership	-	
17. Commercial and Rental Properties (mkt value)		
18. Other Investments (IRA / 401(k) / Keough / ESOP)	56,000	
19. Total Investments	93,500	(19/32) = 13.1%
20. Retirement Funds: Pension (present value)	40,000	
21. Employee Savings Accounts	30,000	
22. Other Long Term Retirement Plans	-	
23. Total Retirement	70,000	(23/32) = 9.8%
24. Personal Property: Prime Residence	375,000	
25. Second Residence / Vacation Home	-	
26. Home Furnishing	50,000	
27. Jewelry	37,500	
28. Collectibles / Art / Antiques	-	
29. Automobiles / Trucks	37,500	
30. Other Assets		
31. Total Personal Property	500,000	(31/32) = 70.0%
32. TOTAL ASSETS	714,500	100.0%

* Disclaimer: This Worksheet is for information purposes only and does not purport to give investment, tax or any other specialized advice. The author does not accept any responsibility or liability for errors or inaccuracies made by users.

ITEM #6. Balance Sheet sample (A2)

LIABILITIES AND OBLIGATIONS
The things I owe others

	SR	% of Liabilities
33. Charge Account Balances / Dept. Stores	-	0.0%
34. Credit Card Balances	22,500	10.5%
35. Personal Loans / Debts	-	0.0%
36. Student Loans	-	0.0%
37. Auto Loans / Leases	4,000	1.9%
38. Pension Loans	-	0.0%
39. Investment Loans (shares/real estate)	-	0.0%
40. Home Mortgage or Lease	188,000	87.6%
41. Home Equity Loans / Second Mortgages	-	0.0%
42. Alimony / Child Support	-	0.0%
43. Life Insurance Policy Loans	-	0.0%
44. Income Tax Liabilities (if any)	-	0.0%
45. Other Obligations / Debts	-	0.0%
46. **TOTAL LIABILITIES**	214,500	100.0%
47. **FINANCIAL NET WORTH**	500,000	= (32-46)

(Assets minus Liabilities)

This is Your Starting Point for a **Personal Wealth Plan**.

ITEM #7. Balance Sheet Blank worksheet (A)

BALANCE SHEET

ASSETS The things that I own	2006 $$	% of Assets
1. Savings: Cash	-	
2. Checking Accounts	-	
3. Money Market Accounts	-	
4. Money Market Funds	-	
5. Certificates of Deposit	-	
6. Gold / Commodities (Mkt value)	-	
7. Mudarabahs	-	
8. Treasury Notes/Bills	-	
9. Cash Value of Life Insurance	-	
10. Total Current Assets	-	
11. Investments: Stocks/Shares	-	
12. Bonds/Soukuks	-	
13. Mutual Funds (current mkt value)	-	
14. Hajj / Umrah Savings Account	-	
15. Partnership Interests	-	
16. Business Enterprise Ownership	-	
17. Commercial and Rental Properties (mkt value)	-	
18. Other Investments (IRA / 401(k) / Keough / ESOP)	-	
19. Total Investments	-	
20. Retirement Funds: Pension (present value)	-	
21. Employee Savings Accounts	-	
22. Other Long Term Retirement Plans	-	
23. Total Retirement	-	
24. Personal Property: Prime Residence	-	
25. Second Residence / Vacation Home	-	
26. Home Furnishing	-	
27. Jewelry	-	
28. Collectibles / Art / Antiques	-	
29. Automobiles / Trucks	-	
30. Other Assets		
31. Total Personal Property		
32. **TOTAL ASSETS**	-	

* *Disclaimer: This Worksheet is for information purposes only and does not purport to give investment, tax or any other specialized advice. The author does not accept any responsibility or liability for errors or inaccuracies made by users.*

ITEM #7. Balance Sheet Blank worksheet (B)

LIABILITIES AND OBLIGATIONS
The things I owe others

	$$	% of Liabilities
33. Charge Account Balances / Dept. Stores	-	
34. Credit Card Balances	-	
35. Personal Loans / Debts	-	
36. Student Loans	-	
37. Auto Loans / Leases	-	
38. Pension Loans	-	
39. Investment Loans (shares/real estate)	-	
40. Home Mortgage or Lease	-	
41. Home Equity Loans / Second Mortgages	-	
42. Alimony / Child Support	-	
43. Life Insurance Policy Loans	-	
44. Income Tax Liabilities (if any)	-	
45. Other Obligations / Debts	-	
46. TOTAL LIABILITIES	-	
47. FINANCIAL NET WORTH	-	

(Assets minus Liabilities)

This is Your Starting Point for a **Personal Wealth Plan**.

ITEM #8. Cash flow Sample worksheet (A1)

CASH FLOW ANALYSIS: MONTHLY BUDGET (WORKSHEET)
Client Name:

INCOME
SOURCES

	Inputs Values		% of Income		
Periodic or Fixed:					
Salary / Earnings - Earner 1	25,000				
Earner 2	-				
Rents and Royalties	-				
Pension Income	-				
Trust Income	-				
Stipends	-				
SubTotal:	25,000		7.4%		
Seasonal or Variable					
Self-Employment Income	-				
Production / Bonuses	15,000				
Vacation / Ramadan Bonus	25,000				
Commissions	-				
SubTotal:	40,000		11.8%		
Savings / Investment Income					
Dividends	-				
Capital Gains	-				
Interest Earnings *	-				
Other Income	-				
SubTotal:	-		0.0%		
Total Cash Available	25,000		19.1%	340,000	Annual

USES
Periodic or Fixed: *Remember inputs from MoExpSheet!*

Housing / Prime / Secondary	8,850		
Insurance Premiums / Property	200		
Insurance Premiums / Personal	1,090	10,140	Subtotal

Seasonal or Variable

Food / Groceries	4,000		
Transportation - Commuting	2,000		
Debt - Obligations Payments	1,000		
Provision for Income Taxes (if any)			
Education (current expenses)	3,300		
Charitable Donations - Good Deeds	360		
Other Personal Items	-		
Other Monthly Expenses / Savings (less Insur prem)	1,800	8,460	Subtotal

Total Expenses	22,600		271,200	Annual
Net Cash Flow: Monthly Surplus (Inflow +/ Outflow-)	2,400		68,800	Annual

* Disclaimer: This Worksheet is for information purposes only and does not purport to give investment, tax or any other specialized advice. The author does not accept any responsibility or liability for errors or inaccuracies made by users.

ITEM #8. Cashflow blank (B1)

CASH FLOW ANALYSIS: MONTHLY BUDGET (FINAL)
Client Name:

INCOME
SOURCES

	Inputs Values	% of Income		
Periodic or Fixed:				
Salary / Earnings - Earner 1	-			
Earner 2	-			
Rents and Royalties	-			
Pension Income	-			
Trust Income	-			
Stipends	-			
SubTotal:	-			
Seasonal or Variable				
Self-Employment Income	-			
Production / Bonuses	-			
Vacation / Ramadan Bonus	-			
Commissions	-			
SubTotal:	-			
Savings / Investment Income				
Dividends	-			
Capital Gains	-			
Interest Earnings *	-			
Other Income	-			
SubTotal:	-	-		
Total Cash Available	-		-	Annual

USES

Periodic or Fixed:	*Remember inputs from MoExpSheet!*			
Housing / Prime / Secondary	-			
Insurance Premiums / Property	-			
Insurance Premiums / Personal	-	-	Subtotal	
Seasonal or Variable				
Food / Groceries	-			
Transportation - Commuting	-			
Debt - Obligations Payments	-			
Provision for Income Taxes (if any)	-			
Education (current expenses)	-			
Charitable Donations - Good Deeds	-			
Other Personal Items	-			
Other Monthly Expenses / Savings (less Insur prem)	-	-	Subtotal	
Total Expenses	-		-	Annual
Net Cash Flow: Monthly Surplus (Inflow +/ Outflow-)	-		-	Annual

ITEM #8 Cashflow sample INPUT worksheets (A2)

SUMMARY REPORT (WORKSHEET)

EXPENSES CATEGORIES

		Monthly	% of Mo. Expenses
Food (groceries)		4,000	17.7%
Housing Expenses	see below	8,850	39.2%
Transportation	see below	2,000	8.8%
Education - School Fees	see below	3,300	14.6%
Charity - Donations		360	1.6%
Other Expenses / Insurance / Savings		3,090	13.7%
Debt / Obligations Payments		1,000	4.4%
Total Monthly Expenses		**22,600**	**100.0%**

HOUSING EXPENSES

	Monthly
Housing Payment / Rental / Lease	4,100
Primary Residence	-
Secondary Residence	-
Real Estate - Property Taxes	-
Utilities (elec / gas)	700
Water - Sewer	200
Telephone	600
Repair / Maintenance	200
Landscaping / Gardening	-
Drivers	1,200
Maids / Servants	800
Other Housing Expenses / Furnishing	1,050
Total Housing Expenses	**8,850**

TRANSPORTATION EXPENSES

Vehicle Payment / Lease	1,250
Vehicle Gas / Oil	250
Vehicle Repairs / Maintenance	300
Other Transportation Exp.	200
Total Transportation Expenses	**2,000**

EDUCATION - SCHOOL FEES*

	Child No. 1	Child No. 2	Child No. 3	Child No. 4	Child No. 5
School Name:	Minerat	DayCare			
Grade:	9	3	0	0	0
Fees Paid Monthly: SR	1800	1500	0	0	0
Total Education Expenses					**3300**

* Include College or University Payments for the current year only here.

ITEM #8 Cashflow INPUT blank (B2)

SUMMARY REPORT (FINAL)

		EXPENSES CATEGORIES	
		Monthly	% of Mo. Expenses
Food (groceries)		-	
Housing Expenses	*see below*	-	
Transportation	*see below*	-	
Education - School Fees	*see below*	-	
Charity - Donations		-	
Other Expenses / Insurance / Savings		-	
Debt / Obligations Payments		-	
Total Monthly Expenses		-	

HOUSING EXPENSES

	Monthly
Housing Payment / Rental / Lease	-
Primary Residence	-
Secondary Residence	-
Real Estate - Property Taxes	-
Utilities (elec / gas)	-
Water - Sewer	-
Telephone	-
Repair / Maintenance	-
Landscaping / Gardening	-
Drivers	-
Maids / Servants	-
Other Housing Expenses / Furnishing	-
Total Housing Expenses	-

TRANSPORTATION EXPENSES

Vehicle Payment / Lease	-
Vehicle Gas / Oil	-
Vehicle Repairs / Miantenance	-
Other Transportation Exp.	-
Total Transportation Expenses	-

EDUCATION - SCHOOL FEES*

	Child No. 1	Child No. 2	Child No. 3	Child No. 4	Child No. 5
School Name:					
Grade:					
Fees Paid Monthly: SR					
Total Education Expenses					

* Include College or University Payments for the current year only here.

ITEM #8 Cashflow sample INPUT worksheets (A3)

OTHER MONTHLY EXPENSES (WORKSHEET)

	Monthly
Clothing / Personal	500
Entertainment / Recreation	200
Day Care - Children	-
Child Support	-
Medical / Dental / Health out of Pocket	100
Insurance / Savings:	
Takaful / Life	-
Disability	-
Waqf / Trust	-
Retirement Plan	1,000
GOSI / Social Security	-
Health / Medical	90
Homeowners / Property	-
Auto /Truck Insurance	200
Other Insurance	-
Emergency Fund	-
Savings Fund	1,000
Education Fund	-
Total Other Expenses	**3,090**

CHARITABLE AND GOOD DEEDS

Gifts	60
Donations	100
Hajj - Umrah Fund	-
Waqf Fund	-
Zakat Contribution	200
Total Charitable Contributions	**360**

DEBT AND OBLIGATION PAYMENTS

Credit cards	1,000
Personal Loans / Leases	-
Other	-
Total Debt Payments	**1,000**

ITEM #8 Cashflow sample INPUT blank (B3)

OTHER MONTHLY EXPENSES (FINAL)

                                                            Monthly

Clothing / Personal
Entertainment / Recreation
Day Care - Children
Child Support
Medical / Dental / Health out of Pocket
Insurance / Savings:
    Takaful / Life
    Disability
    Waqf / Trust
    Retirement Plan
    GOSI / Social Security
    Health / Medical
    Homeowners / Property
    Auto /Truck Insurance
    Other Insurance
Emergency Fund
Savings Fund
Education Fund
        Total Other Expenses

CHARITABLE AND GOOD DEEDS

Gifts
Donations
Hajj - Umrah Fund
Waqf Fund
Zakat Contribution
        Total Charitable Contributions

DEBT AND OBLIGATION PAYMENTS

Credit cards
Personal Loans / Leases
Other
        Total Debt Payments

ITEM #8 Cashflow sample INPUT worksheets (A4)

KEY FINANCIAL INDICATORS (WORKSHEET)
Name

	Monthly	% of Income
Total income	25,000	
Monthly Budget Surplus	2,400	9.6%
Savings / Investments	2,400	8.0%
Other Income / Capital Gains	-	
Total	2,000	
Housing Payments / Rental	4,100	16.4%
Vehicle Lease / Loan	1,250	5.0%
Credit Cards / Personal Loans	1,000	4.0%
Other Leases / Loans	-	0.0%
Total	6,350	
Taxes	-	0.0%
Charities - Donations	360	1.4%
Total	360	

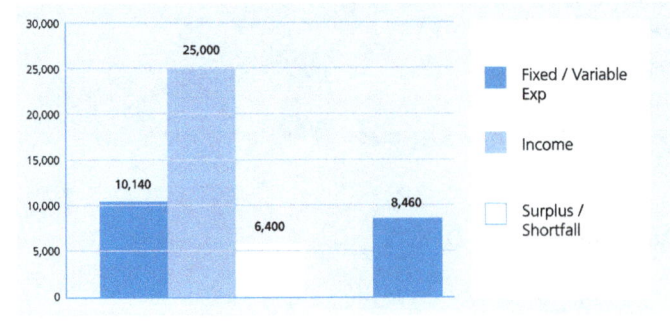

MONTHLY CASH FLOW

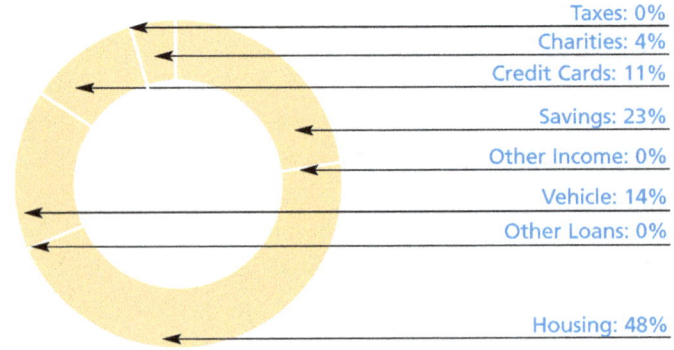

KEY FINANCIAL INDICATORS: MONTHLY

Taxes: 0%
Charities: 4%
Credit Cards: 11%
Savings: 23%
Other Income: 0%
Vehicle: 14%
Other Loans: 0%
Housing: 48%

CONSCIOUS WEALTH

ITEM #8 Cashflow sample INPUT blank (B4)

KEY FINANCIAL INDICATORS (FINAL)
Name:

	Monthly	% of Income
Total income		
Monthly Budget Surplus		
Savings / Investments		
Other Income / Capital Gains		
Total		
Housing Payments / Rental		
Vehicle Lease / Loan		
Credit Cards / Personal Loans		
Other Leases / Loans		
Total		
Taxes		
Charities - Donations		
Total		

MONTHLY CASH FLOW

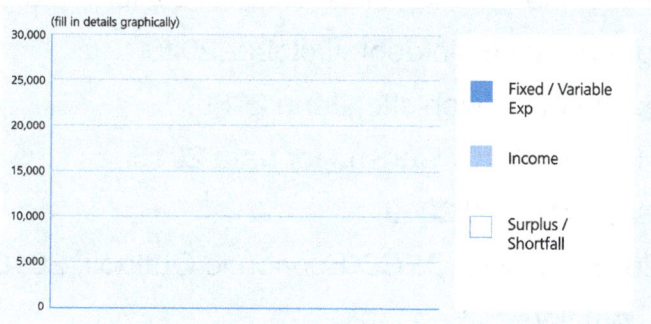

KEY FINANCIAL INDICATORS: MONTHLY

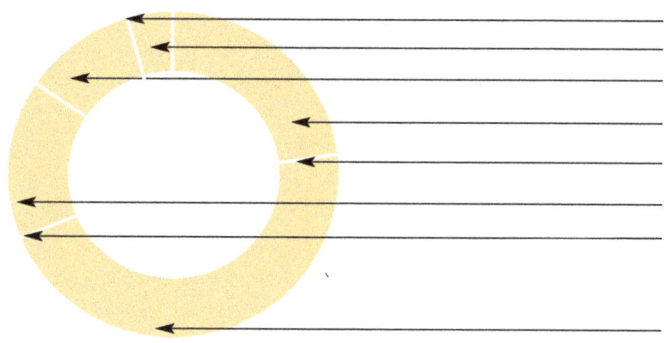

Web Resources Links

- www.calculatorsoup.com
- www.calculator.net
- www.islamreligion.com
- www.isdb.org
- www.slideshare.net // to Dr. Muhammed Yunus interpretation of Imam Al-Ghazali writing
- www.360financialliteracy.org
- www.practicalmoneyskills.ca
- www.oberlo.com
- www.smartmoney.org
- www.slideshare.net
- www.twopaths/com/faq money : resource on Biblical references to money
- www.Debt.org, Americans in debt, October 2020
- Arab Neurology Internet web site, June 2000.
- U.S. Census Bureau, 2015 Census for data 2015.
- www.Geoba.se, 2015 and 2019.
- SIGMA 4/2020, Swiss RE, OECD Economic Outlook, 2018 and WHO
- www.statista.com figures Feb 2020.
- www.ConsciousWealth.me – resources for personal financial intelligence

Reports and Articles

American Savings Education Council Survey, 2001.

Cryptocurrency Spot Exchange Industry Annual Report, Jan 2020, Token Insight.com.

Crowdfunding Global Report, Valuates Reports and QY Research, 2019.

Databrick CEO Nakai's comment in Five Predictions for the Future of Money, source Raconteur. net, 2020

Eureka Hedge article in 2011 describes ISDA/IIFM collaboration to develop a risk hedging mechanism.

Federal Reserve Economic Reports, August 2014/September 2020

Fintech Magazine, Aug. 2020

Fisher, Dr. Omar white paper on "How to Adopt Prosperity Thinking", 2019.

Gallup-Healthways Global Well-Being Index Report 2019, p.4 published Feb. 2020

Gallup "Global Wellbeing- Behavioral Economics of GDP Growth", reports 2020 and 2019, Gallup Inc., New York, USA various polls and reports

Gilad, Sandy paper on "10X Your Happiness", 2015.

GOSI Annual Report, 2019 November, KSA.

GFK Financial Worldwide Survey, June 2012

Helliwell, John F., Editor, Sachs, Jeffrey D.,Layard, Richard, and De Neve, Jan Emmanuel, "World Happiness Report 2020", Sustainable Development Solutions Network, UN New York, 2020 and 2019

OECD Economic Outlook 2019 and Global Finance magazine.

Peerce, Marisa worksheet on "5 Steps to Practice Abundance Thinking", 2020.

Reports by International Bank of Settlements, Hague.

Research from Cap-Gemini Research Institute's World Wealth Report 2020 and Oxfam Report 2014.

Wall Street Journal Survey, June 2001

World Wealth Report 2020, Merrill Lynch Cap Gemini, www.cnbc.com.

U.S. Census Bureau and Bankrate.com, July 2014/ Oct 2020

Bibliography

Alam Choudhury, Prof., "Dispensation of Wealth in Islam", Muscat, Oman 2005.

Al-Ghazali, Imam's writings on slides from Dr. Muhammed Yunus, Prof. at Florida State University, www.slideshare.net, 2015.

Al Maktoum, Sh. Mohammed Bin, "Reflections on Happiness and Positivity", Explorer Publishing, Dubai, 2017

Al Qaradawi, Yusuf, Dr. "Wealth and Economy in Islam", Islamic Inc Publishing, Cairo 2003

Aristotle's treatise Nicomanchaean Ethics, p. 1097 as per www.happinessinternational.org internet, 2015.

Billah Mohd Ma'sum, "Shariah Model of Quantum of Damages in Takaful", IIU, Kuala Lumpur, Malaysia, 2001.

Billah Mohd Ma'sum "Islamic Law of Trade and Finance- Contemporary Issues", IIU, Kuala Lumpur, Malaysia, 2001.

Canfield, Jack, "The Success Principles", HarperElement, 2015

Chopra, Deepak, "The Seven Spiritual Laws of Success", Amber-Allen Publishing, New World Library, 1994

Chopra, Deepak, "Creating Affluence- A-Z Steps to a Richer Life", Amber-Allen Publishing, New World Library, 1994

Choudhury, Masudul Adam, Islam, Mazhar, and Hoq, Ziaul, "The Formation and Valuation of Wealth in Islam," paper, Conference on Wealth Creation in Islam, Durham University, July 2003, page 7.

Christensen, Clayton, "How will you measure your Life?" HarperColins, New York 1012

Conwell, Russel H., "Acres of Diamonds", Project Gutenberg EBooks, Philadelphia, USA, 2008.

Complete Idiot's Guide, Buying Insurance and Annuities, Alpha Books, New York, 1996.

189Crosson, Russ, "Your Money Made Simple- Key to Financial Freedom", Harvest House Publications, Oregon, 2019

Dominguez Joe and Robin Vicki, "Your Money or Your Life", Penguin Books, New

York, 1998.

Edelman Ric, "The Truth About Money", Harper Business Series, New York, 1998.

Ernest & Young, "Financial Planning Essentials," Wiley & Sons, New York, 1999.

ETHICA Institute, "Zakat Q and A Handbook", 2013 published in Dubai, UAE as EBook.

Federal Reserve Bank of Dallas, "Building Wealth- a Beginner's Guide to Securing Your Financial future", July 2003.

Feigenbaum Alan, "Retirement planning", Alpha Books, New York, 2002.

Fisher, Mark and Allen, Marc, "How to Think like a Millionaire", New World Library, Calif 1997

Fisher, Dr. Omar, "A Takaful Primer", publication with Thomson Reuters to World Takaful Conference- Dubai, 2013.

Fisher, Dr. Omar "Conscious Wealth Guide to Financial Intelligence- Faith and Money in 21st Century", Xlibrius 2021.

Franklin, Benjamin, "The Way to Wealth", Applewood Books, 1986

Hamerman, F. William, "The Road to Happiness", Al Muntada Al Islami, 2001, Riyadh Hill, Napoleon, "Think and Grow Rich" (1937).

Iqbal, Zamir and Mirakhor, Abbas, "An Introduction to Islamic Finance- Theory and Practice", John Wiley & Sons, USA, 2007

INCEIF, "Man's Right to Wealth", reprint in Malaysia, 2013.

"Islamic Financial system- Elimination of Riba," IIU, Kuala Lumpur, Malaysia, June 1997.

Khan M. Muhsin, Dr. and Al Hilali M. Taqi-ud-Din, Dr., "Translation of the Meaning of the Noble Quran", Riyadh 1996.

Klein, Stefan, Dr. "The Science of Happiness: How our brains make us happy", Scribe 2002

McKenna, Paul, "I Can Make You Rich", Bantum Press, Great Britain, 2007

Mills, Paul, "The Great Financial Crisis: a Biblical Diagnosis", Cambridge Papers, Vol.20, No.1, March 2011, Jubilee Centre, Cambridge, UK.

Morris Kenneth, and Morris Virginia, "Guide to Planning Your Financial Future,"

Wall St. Journal, Lightbulb Press and Dow Jones, New York, 1998.

Morris Virginia and Ingram Brian, "Guide to Understanding Islamic Investing", Lightbulb Press and Dow Jones, New York, 2001.

190Morris Kenneth and Morris Virginia, "Guide to Understanding Personal Finance", Wall Street Journal, Lightbulb Press, New York, 2000.

Murphy, Joseph, Dr. "The Power of your Subconscious Mind", Pocket Book Prentice Hall, UK 2006

Nasser Al-Omar, Dr., "The Road to Happiness", from lectures compiled by F. William Hamerman, Riyadh 2001.

Philips, A.A.B., Dr. "The Purpose of Creation", Dar Al Fatah Press, UAE, 1997

Pickford James, Editor "Mastering Risk- Financial Times Mastering Series", Pearson Ed. Ltd. Press, London, UK, 2001.

Procter, Bob, "You Were Born Rich" (1997)

Proctor, Bob, "The ABCs of Success", Penguin, New York, 2015

Proctor, Bob, "It is Not about the Money", Burman Books, Inc. Toronto, Canada, 2009

Ramsey, Dave, "Total Money Makeover," CD Rom, 2002.

Sander P.J and Sander J.B., "Living on a Budget," The Pocket Idiot's Guide, Alpha Books, IN, USA, 1999.

Saviue, Luminita D., "15 Things you should give up to be Happy", Penguin New York, 2016

Seppala, Emma, Dr., "The Happiness Track: How to apply the Science of Happiness", HarperOne, 2017

Scott, Steven K., "Millionaire's Notebook", Simon & Schuster, New York 1996

Stanley, Thomas J. and Danko, William D., "The Millionaire Next Door", Simon & Schuster, New York 1996

Vicary Abdullah, Daud and Chee, Keon, "Islamic Finance – Why it makes sense", Marshall Cavendish International, Singapore, 2010

Wall Street Journal, "Guide to Understanding Personal Finance," p. 125.

Wattles, Wallace D., "The Science of Getting Rich", Destiny Books, Vermont, 2007

World Bank, Development Report 2004, 2013 and WHO.

World Bank, New Ideas About Old Age Security, Washington, DC (2000)

Index

A

abundance - 20, 21, 74, 83, 84, 125, 181

abundance mindset - 38, 126, 166, 186

abundance thinking - 24-29, 34, 37-40, 73, 120-122, 181

action agenda - 19, 23-25, 29, 215-218, 220-222, 228, 234

action learning project - 21, 28

ambition - 51

asset - 19-20, 24-25, 31, 34-36, 40, 62, 75, 80, 92, 95-99, 111, 138, 140-143, 146, 154-156, 161, 168, 182-183, 190-192, 198, 200-201, 206, 220-221, 231

attitude - 24, 50-52, 55, 84, 120, 126-127, 168, 170-172, 181-183, 196, 218

awareness - 18, 21, 23-27, 29-30, 39, 55, 57-58, 73, 80, 113-114, 154-155, 167, 185, 187, 221

B

balance sheet - 22, 89-90, 95-99, 101, 140, 142-146, 221, 231, 242-245

basic life skills - 28

being well - 182

belief - 25-26, 45-47, 55, 66-67, 70, 84-87, 126, 153, 170, 175, 180, 212-213, 230

bible - 22, 24, 101, 122, 123

bills - 17, 79, 83, 93, 97, 111, 197-198, 218

bitcoin - 111, 202-204

blueprint - 16, 24, 29

bond - 27, 92, 97, 111, 145, 160, 195-199

budget - 16, 19, 24-25, 29, 63, 71, 74-75, 91, 99, 103-107, 112-115, 140, 144-146, 150-151, 155-156, 194, 201, 211, 220-221, 231, 238, 260

C

cash flow - 74, 76, 89-95, 98, 100-102, 112, 140, 194, 201, 217, 231, 246

charity - 20, 83, 105-106, 110

clarity - 22, 24, 29-30, 40, 49, 53, 58, 75, 86-87, 137, 150, 186, 213, 218, 231

clarity of mind - 49, 58, 86, 137

coaching wheel program - 15-16, 23, 25-27, 30, 40, 83, 119, 186, 227-228

commitment - 23-24, 26, 63, 67, 176, 211, 226-228

conscious wealth - 18, 20-21, 23, 25-30, 36-37, 53, 56, 73-75, 90, 95, 112, 117-118, 122, 127, 184, 186, 227, 231

credit card - 77, 93, 97, 108, 203, 217

cross over point - 81, 150, 152-154, 159, 161

curriculum - 21

D

debt - 16, 19-20, 22, 35-36, 71, 76, 80, 83, 93, 95, 98, 105-109, 122-123, 141-142, 146, 154-157, 193, 218-221, 230, 254

debt-free - 71, 122

decision-making - 15, 38, 52, 138-139, 147

digital money - 28, 182, 202-206

discipline - 51, 99-100, 227

disposable - 91, 100, 141-142, 158, 194, 217

donate - 74-75, 124

dreams - 15, 17, 24, 29, 43, 75, 98, 137, 151, 170, 172, 225

E

earning - 17, 21, 64, 75, 91, 92, 95, 99, 105, 124, 139, 152, 156, 158, 192

emergency fund - 1, 41, 14, 51, 56, 141-145, 156, 191

emotion - 26-27, 45, 49, 73, 87, 134, 137, 139, 172-176, 178, 182, 185

empower - 70, 85, 87, 90, 227

equity - 97-98, 108, 111, 145, 193, 195, 200

exercises - 15-17, 21-29, 36, 39-40, 50-52, 64-65, 67, 70-72, 79, 85, 87, 94, 98-99, 112, 119, 126, 136-137, 140, 151, 155, 161-162, 190, 198-201, 206, 211-212, 217, 227, 230-231

F

failure - 39, 51-53, 57, 114, 159, 166-172, 186, 203, 222

faith - 18-24, 37, 46-47, 62, 117-119, 124, 192, 225, 231, 258

financial freedom - 17, 19, 23-25, 38, 80-81, 90, 113, 122, 149-163, 200, 231

financial intelligence - 15-21, 25-26, 30, 75, 186, 231-232, 254

financial journey - 29

financial literacy - 20, 28, 231

finlit - 20, 28

G

gap analysis - 61, 63-65, 67, 209-211

gaps - 24-25, 29, 39, 61-70, 161-162, 209-214

gifts - 19, 25, 34-35, 40, 51, 62, 92, 101, 105, 110, 119, 126, 175, 192, 231

goals - 15-17, 19, 23-29, 34, 37, 44, 49, 56, 62, 67, 75, 80, 83, 95, 98, 100, 103, 121-123, 129-139, 145, 147, 152, 154-156, 167-168, 171-172, 175-176, 180, 183-184, 192-196, 200, 213, 217-218, 220, 225, 227, 231

H

habit - 17, 19-23, 26, 30, 39-40, 45, 52-53, 55, 57, 80, 99, 112-113, 124, 139-140, 146, 172, 175, 182, 185,

199, 201, 219, 221, 231

happiness - 5, 15, 17, 19, 23-27, 29, 37, 39-40, 73, 83-84, 90, 122, 156, 159, 165-166, 173-182, 185-187, 210, 213, 231, 255, 257-260

healthy money habit - 26, 30, 55, 100, 175, 181, 199, 231

high achiever - 37, 53

high points - 30, 39-40, 58, 67, 87, 101, 114, 127, 147, 163, 186, 206, 213, 222, 228

I

income - 22, 25, 38, 63-65, 74, 75, 81, 88-95, 97, 99-101, 105-110, 112, 122-124, 138-146, 153-158, 161, 192,-194, 199-200, 221, 231,

income statement - 22, 90, 101, 140-146, 221, 231

inflation - 100, 138, 162, 182

inheritance - 92, 101, 105, 107, 124, 191-193

insurance - 16, 27, 77, 79, 92-94, 97-98, 105-107, 111, 141, 144, 192, 199, 258

interest - 93-94, 97, 107-109, 146, 198, 200

inventory - 19, 25, 33-35, 40, 62, 156, 221, 231

investing - 18-19, 24-26, 29, 73, 91, 99, 111, 118, 139, 141, 145, 182, 189, 197-200, 218, 220, 259

investment - 5, 7, 16, 19, 23-24, 63, 76-77, 81, 92-97, 100, 104-111, 138-143, 147, 152-156, 160, 190-206, 211, 217, 221, 225

islamic - 20, 76, 78, 109, 124, 200, 257, 259-260

K

knowledge - 15, 17, 23, 25, 38, 48, 67, 73, 99, 105, 107, 110, 119, 124-126, 167, 171, 175, 192, 219, 231

L

law of attraction - 38, 66, 212

learning - 16-30, 34, 37-40, 44, 48, 54-58, 62, 67, 73, 79, 87, 91, 93, 101, 110-114, 118, 127, 147, 150, 159, 163, 170-174, 183, 186, 198, 201, 204, 206, 213, 219-222, 226, 228

liabilities - 19, 24, 35-36, 95-99, 108, 142, 146, 156, 221, 231

lifestyle - 17, 19, 23-25, 107, 138, 145, 149-152, 161-166

liquidity - 76, 138, 141, 146, 156, 195, 220

loan - 35-36, 80, 97-98, 105-109, 156-159, 217, 219

love - 3, 61, 83-84, 101, 120, 123, 131, 134, 159, 165, 174, 176, 180

love of money - 83-84

M

magic boxes - 25, 102, 105, 112, 114

master - 21-22, 25-27, 39, 56-57, 77, 114, 122, 186, 222, 260

mastery - 25, 27, 122

mental - 16, 27, 44-45, 48-54, 82-86, 135, 159, 169, 172, 177, 213, 231

mindset - 15, 22, 38, 52, 70, 82-84, 87, 126, 166, 181, 183, 186-187

mission - 231

money EQ - 73-74

money habits - 19, 23, 30, 112, 139-140, 146, 201, 231

money IQ - 73-74, 82-83

money mood - 82

mutual - 16, 27, 97, 160, 196, 199-200

N

net worth - 22, 88, 90, 95-99, 101, 141-143, 154-156, 200

P

paradigm - 54-58, 120, 172, 178-181, 213, 231

passive income - 97, 107, 139, 161, 200

pedagogy - 21, 30, 186

performance - 27, 40, 64, 67, 70, 157, 211, 213

personal success - 16-17, 37, 52, 120, 171, 223

personal wealth plan - 16, 18, 21, 23, 36-37, 95, 98, 199, 227

pledge - 19, 23-25, 29, 34, 225-228

property - 76, 92-93, 97, 105, 111, 120, 192, 195

prosperity - 39, 80, 126, 255

prosperity thinking - 39

protection - 79, 105, 111, 124-125, 138

purpose - 44, 47, 51, 53, 80, 90, 98, 101, 119-120, 124, 127, 136, 175-179, 181-182, 213, 260

PWP - 16, 18, 23-25, 29, 34, 36, 95, 98-100, 226-228

Q

quran - 22, 24, 101, 118, 123-125, 127, 192

R

ratio - 17, 19, 24-27, 29, 129-130, 139-150, 200-201, 231

real wealth - 20, 83, 93, 96, 122, 183, 190-200, 206

retirement - 15, 19, 23-25, 29, 77, 92, 97, 99-100, 105, 111, 118, 138, 141, 145, 149-164, 191, 193, 199, 201, 220, 231, 258

riba - 259

risk - 19-20, 23-29, 34, 46, 76, 79, 84,

100, 105, 109, 111, 118, 138, 145, 174, 189-206, 220-221, 226, 238, 255, 260

roadblocks - 51, 213

roadmap - 17-18, 20-21, 25, 34, 37, 83, 98, 113, 181 ,227, 231

S

saving - 15-19, 24-26, 29, 65, 79-80, 90-91, 93, 97, 99-101, 105-106, 110-112, 139-145, 150, 152-153, 156, 158-159, 162-163, 182, 190-195, 199-201, 206, 217-221, 230-231, 255

scarcity - 83-84, 126, 181

science - 19, 26, 45-48, 166, 174, 180, 186, 259-260

securities - 38, 76, 92, 111, 143, 195, 197, 200

security - 46, 74, 91-97, 120, 161, 204-205, 260

self-actualization - 118-122, 127

self-confidence - 25, 46, 80, 119

self-leadership - 46

solvency - 141-143

soul - 27, 44-45

sources and uses - 71 ,104-105, 114, 240-241

sources of income - 38, 74, 105, 157, 161, 192

sources of money - 105

spirit - 47-49, 65, 122, 181

spiritual - 18, 20, 25, 27, 40, 47-49, 65, 107, 122, 126, 168, 177, 180-181, 257

starting point - 25, 29-30, 44-45, 95, 98, 156, 180, 217, 219,

success - 15-20, 28, 37, 46, 52, 56-58, 62, 91, 96, 112-113, 118-120, 127, 154-155, 165-166, 172, 181-186, 199, 210, 213, 221, 231, 257, 260

success principles - 56, 58, 184, 257

sukuk - 111, 195

T

takaful - 257-258

thinking - 26, 30, 33, 37, 43-46, 49-50, 53-55, 58, 66, 84, 126, 178, 181, 183-184, 187, 212-213

thinking into results - 46, 53, 58, 213

threats to saving - 99

tips - 15, 37, 90, 94, 100-101, 107-111, 122, 166, 185-186, 194

tokens - 20, 111, 255

traps - 70, 83-84, 87

U

universal law - 47-48, 50, 66, 123, 192, 212, 257

universe - 48, 126 169, 175, 181

uses (financial) - 71, 104-110, 114, 240-241

uses of money - 104-105, 114

W

wealth - 7, 15-17, 19-31, 34, 36-37, 53, 56-57, 73-77, 79-83, 93, 95-98, 100-101, 112, 117-119, 122-128, 138, 142-145, 150-152, 158-159, 163, 175, 181, 183-184, 186, 190-201, 206, 220-221, 227, 231-232, 256-259

wealth accumulation - 124-125

wealth distribution - 124-125, 158

wealth preservation - 124-125

wealth purification - 124-125

wealth report - 158-159, 256

wealth-building - 15, 20, 24, 79-80, 122, 124, 143, 193, 195, 197

well-being - 15-17, 80, 84, 93, 122, 126, 166, 178-179, 181-182, 185-186, 255

wheel of life - 70-72, 87

winning - 92, 105, 107, 168, 191

wishful thinking - 63, 211

CPSIA information can be obtained
at www.ICGtesting.com
Printed in the USA
BVHW011536220922
647764BV00009B/228